Conversation Pieces
in Everyday English

BOOK II

M. F. Jerrom
and
L. L. Szkutnik

Illustrated by Michael ffolkes

LONGMAN

LONGMAN GROUP LIMITED
Longman House, Burnt Mill, Harlow,
Essex CM20 2JE, England
and Associated Companies throughout the world.

*First published *1965*
*Reprinted *1985*

ISBN 0 582 52388 5

Produced by Longman Group (FE) Limited
Printed in Hong Kong

Foreword

This second volume of *Conversation Exercises in Everyday English* contains more advanced constructions than the first volume. Otherwise it is of similar plan, except that from page 131 onwards there are longer conversations in special situations.

The principles on which the book is based, as set out in the Foreword to Book One, are restated here. The books are designed to help learners who wish to speak the language well, but they are also useful to those whose aim is to read English, as learning to speak is the best way of mastering the fundamentals.

The quickest way of learning to speak is to practise and practise speaking with such frequent repetition as to form habits of correct expression. This is much more important than the learning of descriptive grammar and vocabulary.

In this belief, the aim of this book is to help the teacher and the learner by providing a large number of ready-made conversations, and so to avoid the waste of time so common in classrooms when the 'conversation lesson' takes place, often a time of improvised questions and faltering, frequently incorrect answers, punctuated by uneasy silences. The correct use of the book will ensure that all members of the class have ample practice in speaking, without hearing incorrect constructions.

Experience has shown that, using the exercises, every member of the class can speak a large number of times during the lesson, and it is hoped that the book will thus prove a valuable aid to courses in the English language. The same dialogues can be turned to again and again until they become familiar, and so the students acquire command of the functional grammar of the language without conscious effort.

The plan is based on the grading of verbal constructions, which are the backbone of the language. Although it is not the intention to provide a complete course, most of the common constructions are included, and a large number of everyday words as well. The index will help the teacher to choose the exercises required.

Tape recordings are available with this book, and a note on their use can be found on page vi .

iii

Guide to using this book

As in Book One, each page gives two set dialogues illustrating a particular construction, followed by a PRACTICE dialogue 'frame' of the same type with numbered gaps into which pupils can put suitable words and phrases taken from the numbered ists (or substitution tables) below. The numbers of the gaps refer to the numbers of the lists.

In the PRACTICE dialogues one oblique stroke indicates a choice of single words, two oblique strokes a choice of word groups; e.g. last summer/Christmas holiday; Yes, I expect so//No, I don't think so. Sometimes, in more complicated constructions, brackets are used to indicate a choice; e.g.:

$$\text{Probably because} \left\{ \begin{array}{l} \text{he/she hasn't} \\ \text{they haven't} \end{array} \right\} \text{been } \ldots \text{ 1+ing}$$

Some words in the dialogues and lists are in brackets, to show that they are required in particular constructions only, or in a few cases are optional additions.

It is suggested that:

(1) The teacher, having chosen the appropriate exercise, gets the class to repeat after him the set dialogues.

(2) Then, the class having been paired off, the pairs in turn read the dialogue round the class.

(3) Next, the class repeats a number of variations chosen by the teacher from the given lists.

(4) The pairs then repeat the substitution dialogue without the aid of the teacher, choosing their own variations from the lists.

Suppose, for example, the class is working the dialogues on page 31, the use of the Present Tense indicating future after 'if', etc.

iv

After carrying out (1), (2) and (3) above, attention passes to the dialogue frame and tables, as follows:

A: If it's a nice day tomorrow, I'll . . . **1.**
B: And if it isn't nice?
A: If it isn't nice, I'll . . . **1a.**
B: So shall I.

1.
take my wife for a drive
       family for a picnic
do some sailing
    skiing
    gardening
go to the football match
  on the river
  fishing
  swimming
prune the roses
have a walk in the woods

1a.
clean the car
arrange my stamps
play the gramophone
    chess
listen to some records
read a novel
have a quiet day
work in the greenhouse
    on my book

The first pair have a number of choices, and perhaps the dialogue goes like this:

A: If it's a nice day tomorrow, I'll do some sailing.
B: And if it isn't nice?
A: If it isn't nice, I'll clean the car.
B: So shall I.

The next pair may continue:

A: If it's a nice day tomorrow, I'll take the family for a picnic.
B: And if it isn't nice?
A: If it isn't nice, I'll play chess.
B: So shall I.

And so on round the class.

This procedure allows for a great variety of dialogues and gives students some freedom of choice of meaning, without choice of construction. This limited freedom of choice (and the occasional ill-assorted meanings that will arise) should be sufficient to prevent monotony.

The dialogues can also be very useful for private students, especially when working in pairs.

The classifications and the choice of numbers are the same as in Book One, with two additions. They do not pretend to be anything more than a practical aid, as follows:

XYZ Proper names
1. Infinitive without 'to'
2. Preterite
3. Past participle
4. Adjectival elements
5. Noun elements
6. Modifiers of time
7. Modifiers of place
8. Modifiers of frequency
9. Clauses and longer constructions

USE OF THE TAPE RECORDINGS

In Class. The teacher should first allow the class to listen to the spoken dialogue while looking at the text in their books. The class should repeat the dialogue in the pauses provided in the second reading—first together, and then on subsequent playings individually or in pairs as the teacher directs, the teacher stopping the recorder and winding back the tape for replaying a number of times until the dialogue is sufficiently familiar. The class can then proceed to deal with the second set dialogue and the practice dialogue as recommended above.

Individual students. With students working alone, in pairs or in the language laboratory, the same procedure can be used, the student stopping and winding back the tape for replaying until the dialogue has been sufficiently practised.

Note. On the accompanying tapes, dialogues are recorded up to and including page 125, but *not* for pages 126 to the end of the book. Normally the first set dialogue is recorded but where the second dialogue is recorded instead (i.e. on pages 6, 21, 34, 36, 39, 51, 60, 62, 67, 76, 82, 90, 103, 109, 112, and 118), this is indicated by an asterisk after the title at the head of the page. On page 28 both dialogues are recorded; neither of the dialogues on page 29 is recorded; this is indicated by a footnote in each case.

Contents

Bill can swim well. So can Jack

A : Bill is very athletic. He can
     swim very well.
B : So can Jack.
A : Yes, they are both very
     good at sport.
B : So are the Wood brothers.

A : Kate is very athletic. She
     can run like the wind.
B : So can Mary.
A : Yes, they are both very
     good at sport.
B : So are the Wood sisters.

PRACTICE

A : **X** is very athletic. He/She
     can **. . . 1**.
B : So can **Y**.
A : Yes, they are both very
     good at sport.
B : So are the Wood brothers/
     sisters.

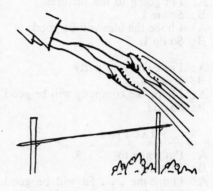

. . . jump very high.

1

jump very high
run for miles
play tennis extremely well
    football
    hockey
    most games well
wrestle and box very well
dive beautifully
skate perfectly

So am I

A: I'm going to the pictures.
B: So am I.
A: I hope the film will be good.
B: So do I.

A: I'm going to a party.
B: So am I.
A: I hope the company will be good.
B: So do I.

PRACTICE

A: I'm going to . . . 5.
B: So am I.
A: I hope the . . . 5a will be good.
B: So do I.

5	5a
the theatre	play
concert	music
	singing
circus	animals
	clowns
	acrobats
sports meeting	running
dance	band
a conference	speakers

So has Bill

A : Where's Kate?
B : She's got to stay at home
and look after the children.
A : So has Bill, as a matter of
fact.
B : Then we can't play bridge,
can we?

A : Where's Henry?
B : He's got to stay at home
and do some homework.
A : So has Jane, as a matter of
fact.
B : Then we can't go sailing,
can we?

. . . *read to Granny.*

PRACTICE

A : Where's **X**?
B : He's/She's got to stay at
home and . . . **1**.
A : So has **Y**, as a matter of
fact.
B : Then we can't . . . **1a**, can
we?

1

mind the baby
read to Granny
answer some letters
finish some work
        packing
do some cooking
      mending
   his/her homework
      music practice
finish the accounts
make some jam

1a

play golf
   tennis
   cards
go swimming
   skating
   riding
   to the pictures
   for a walk

3

So did Paul

A: Jim played truant again yesterday.
B: So did Paul.
A: Won't they get into trouble?
B: Yes, I expect so.

A: Alice lost a book again yesterday.
B: So did Vera.
A: Won't they get into trouble?
B: No, I don't think so.

PRACTICE

A: **X . . . 2** again yesterday.
B: So did **Y**.
A: Won't they get into trouble?
B: Yes, I expect so//No, I don't think so.

2

broke a window
       chair
got wet through
     stopped for speeding
came home very late
smashed his/her bicycle
forgot his/her homework
missed his/her English lesson
failed his/her exam
tore his coat//her frock

So ought Jill

A: I'm afraid Jack and Jill aren't getting on very well in English.
B: No, they aren't. Particularly Jack. He ought to work harder.
A: So ought Jill.
B: I quite agree.

A: I'm afraid Jack and Jill aren't getting on very well in biology.
B: No, they aren't. Particularly Jack. He should attend to his lessons better.
A: So should Jill.
B: I quite agree.

. . . aren't getting on very well in biology.

PRACTICE

A: I'm afraid Jack and Jill aren't getting on very well in . . . 5.
B: No, they aren't. Particularly Jack. He ought to/ should . . . 1.
A: So ought/should Jill.
B: I quite agree.

5	1
music	be more careful
physical training	serious
mathematics	steadier
science	do his homework regularly
geography	exercises more carefully
Latin	read more
	change his attitude
	practise harder

5

Neither does Joan*

A : Phyllis doesn't like flowers.
B : Neither does Joan.
A : No. They both prefer vegetables.
B : So does Tom.

A : Henry doesn't like football.
B : Neither does Alfred.
A : No. They both prefer hockey.
B : So does Joan.

PRACTICE

A : **X** doesn't like . . . **5**.
B : Neither does **Y**.
A : No. They both prefer . . . **5**.
B : So does **Z**.

5

tennis	reading novels
golf	singing
gardening	playing the piano
cycling	violin
rowing	cello
sailing	apples
fishing	pears
skiing	

Have you ever been to Australia?

A: Have you ever been to
Australia?
B: No, I haven't.
A: Neither have I, but I've
been to Japan.
B: So have I.

A: Has your father ever been
to sea?
B: No, he hasn't.
A: Neither has mine, but he's
flown the Atlantic.
B: So has mine.

I've been to Japan.

PRACTICE

A: Have you//has your father
ever . . . **3**?
B: No, I haven't//he hasn't.
A: Neither have I//has mine,
but I've/he's . . . **3**.
B: So have I//So has mine.

3

been to Paris   made a parachute descent
         Vienna   worked as a diver
         Oslo   in a factory
         Madrid   on a farm
   in the army   gone mountaineering
         navy   ski-ing
         air force
   a glider
down a mine

Neither am I

A : I'm not going to the club,
    I'm afraid.
B : Neither am I.
A : It's a pity, isn't it?
B : Yes, I suppose so.

A : I mustn't eat sweets, I'm
    afraid.
B : Neither must I.
A : It's a pity, isn't it?
B : Yes, I suppose so.

PRACTICE

A : I . . . **1**, I'm afraid.
B : Neither . . . **1a** I.
A : It's a pity, isn't it?
B : Yes, I suppose so.

. . . don't often go to the art gallery.

1	1a
can't speak Latin fluently	can
haven't got a motor car	have
boat	
don't like modern music	do
often go to the art gallery	
didn't go to the theatre yesterday	did
work very hard yesterday	
oughtn't to drink alcohol	ought
shouldn't go to the dance tonight	should

You mustn't read too much

A : I feel very tired these days.
B : You mustn't read too much.
A : But I don't.
B : And you mustn't stay at home too much, either.

A : Mother feels very tired these days.
B : She mustn't work too hard.
A : You are probably right.
B : And she mustn't do all the washing, either.

PRACTICE

A : I feel ⎱ very tired these days.
    X feels ⎰
B : You/He/She mustn't . . . **1**.
A : You are probably right//But I don't.
B : And you/he/she mustn't . . . **1**, either.

1

go to too many dances
sit up too late
work too hard at night
worry too much
play cards too late
    too much football
do too much digging
          heavy work
drink too much
eat too much

He mustn't waste so much time

A: Tom has had a bad report.
B: Yes. He could do much better.
A: I know. He mustn't waste so much time.
B: And he mustn't stay away from school so often, either.

A: Jane has had a bad report.
B: Yes. She could do much better.
A: I know. She mustn't come so late to class.
B: And she mustn't neglect her homework, either.

. . . sit next to that bad girl.

A: **X** has had a bad report.
B: Yes. He/She could do much better.
A: I know. He/She mustn't . . . **1**.
B: And he/she mustn't . . . **1**, either.

1

go to bed so late
keep such late hours
work so hard outside school
sit next to that bad boy/girl **X**
spend so much time dancing
think only of pop music
write so many letters
read so many comics
          novels
be so hostile to the teacher
10

An expedition to shoot a film

A: My cousin has joined a jungle expedition.
B: What for?
A: To shoot a film about animals.
B: That's very brave of him.

A: A girl friend of mine has joined an Amazon expedition.
B: What for?
A: To study the lives of the native tribes.
B: That's very brave of her.

. . . *a film about animals.*

PRACTICE

A: **X** has joined a (an) **. . . 4** expedition.
B: What for?
A: To **. . . 1**.
B: That's very brave of him/her.

4	1
arctic	hunt big game
desert	tigers
under water	lions
South Seas	elephants
bush	panthers
zoological	white bears
mountaineering	seals
	sharks
	look for gold
	have exciting adventures
	set up a climbing record
	collect snakes
	rare animals

11

A special instrument for measuring depth

A: I've bought a very useful thing.
B: What is it?
A: It's a special instrument for measuring depth.
B: I'd very much like to see it work.

A: I've bought a very useful thing.
B: What is it?
A: It's a special gadget for curling hair.
B: I'd very much like to see it work.

PRACTICE

A: I've bought a very useful thing.
B: What is it?
A: It's a special . . . **5** for . . . **1+ing**.
B: I'd very much like to see it work.

5	**1+ing**
tool	opening tins
container	making tea
pot	coffee
device	cooking meat
substance	developing films
kind of medicine	learning languages
	improving one's memory

Buying a car for pleasure

A: Are you going to buy a car
   soon?
B: Why should I buy a car?
A: For pleasure.
B: Well, I'll have to think
   about it.

A: Are you going to get a
   bicycle soon?
B: Why should I get a bicycle?
A: To save bus fares.
B: Well, I'll have to think
   about it.

. . . buy a yacht.

PRACTICE

A: Are you going to . . . **1**
   soon?
B: Why should I . . . **1**?
A: For . . . **5**.
   To . . . **1a**.
B: Well, I'll have to think
   about it.

1	**5**	**1a**
buy a scooter	the sake of convenience	have a hobby
yacht	fun	have an interest in life
give up your job	safety's sake	
get a radio	X's sake	fun
TV set	reasons of economy	more time to spare
learn to swim	getting the news	economise
sell your car		
horse		spend more time at home
resign from the club		be well informed

I used to go swimming

A: Where did you spend last summer holidays?
B: In the country.
A: What did you do there?
B: Lots of things. I used to go swimming, for instance.

A: Where did you spend last winter holidays?
B: In the mountains.
A: What did you do there?
B: Lots of things. We used to go tobogganing, for example.

PRACTICE

A: Where did you spend last summer / winter holidays?
B: . . . 7.
A: What did you do there?
B: Lots of things. I / We used to . . . 1, for instance / example.

7	1	
on the coast	go	climbing
lakes		fishing
at the seaside		sailing
home		dancing
in Switzerland		mushrooming
Scotland		skiing
		to the theatre
	play	tennis
		football
		volley-ball
		cards
	watch television	
	listen to the radio	
	sit on the beach	
	have picnics	

14

There used to be a pub

A : This village hasn't changed much since last year.

B : Except that there used to be a pub where the library is now.

A : And there's now a butcher's where the grocer's used to be

B : Yes, that's right.

A : This town hasn't changed much since our boyhood.

B : Except that there used to be a field where the new housing estate is now.

A : And there's a bank where the music hall used to be.

B : Yes, that's right.

. . . hasn't changed much since 1900.

PRACTICE

A : This village/town hasn't changed much since . . . **6**.

B : Except that there used to be a . . . **5** where the . . . **5** is now.

A : And there's a . . . **5** where the . . . **5** used to be.

B : Yes, that's right.

6

my childhood
before the war
1900
five years ago
my/your last visit
the war
    First World War

5

chemist's
greengrocer's
baker's
dairy
bookshop
lending library
restaurant
school
row of shops
garage
service station
church
park
bandstand

Jill is to cook the dinner

A: Where are Jack and Jill?
B: Mother said she needed them at home.
A: What for?
B: Jack is to look after the children and Jill is to cook the dinner.

A: Where are Jack and Jill?
B: Mother said she needed them at home.
A: What for?
B: Jack is to work in the garden and Jill is to do the washing up.

PRACTICE

A: Where are Jack and Jill?
B: Mother said she needed them at home.
A: What for?
B: Jack is to . . . 1 and Jill is to . . . 1.

1

make the beds
     a cake
set the table
do the dusting
sweep the floor
take the dog out
mind the baby

clean out the stables
peel the potatoes
fetch the coal
put the toys away
wash the car
help with the washing up
wipe up

Where is the new hotel to be?

A : Where is the new hotel to be?
B : At the corner of Longway and Market Street.
A : I thought there was to be a chapel there.
B : No, the chapel will be further down Market Street.

A : Where is the new super-market to be?
B : At the corner of Broadway and High Street.
A : I thought there was to be a pub there.
B : No, the pub will be further down Broadway.

PRACTICE

A : Where is the new . . . 5 to be?
B : At the corner of . . . **X** and **Y** Street.
A : I thought there was to be a . . . 5 there.
B : No, the . . . 5 will be further down **X** Street / Road.

5

cinema
theatre
bingo hall
garage
service station
bus station
department store
market
civic centre
Town Hall
church
car park
hospital

17

I'll be going to the beach

A: You've missed a lot of
   English classes lately.
B: Yes, I'm afraid so.
A: I hope you'll come to class
   on Tuesday.
B: I'm afraid not. I'll be going
   to the beach on Tuesday.

A: You've missed a lot of
   English classes lately.
B: Yes, I'm afraid so.
A: I hope you'll come to class
   on Monday.
B: I'm afraid not. I'll be hav-
   ing my music lesson on
   Monday.

. . . flying to Monte Carlo.

PRACTICE

A: You've missed a lot of
   English classes lately.
B: Yes, I'm afraid so.
A: I hope you'll come to class
   on . . . **6**.
B: I'm afraid not. I'll be
   . . . **1 + ing** on . . . **6**.

6	1 + ing
Wednesday	playing football
Thursday	tennis
Friday	cards
Saturday	going to the theatre
	concert
	bingo
	flying to Paris
	Monte Carlo
	Edinburgh
	having some visitors to lunch
	tea
	dinner
	decorating our house

18

Will you be passing the grocer's?

A: What's the time?
B: It's five past three.
A: Then I must go to the butcher's.
B: Will you be passing the grocer's on your way?
A: Yes, I will. Do you need anything?
B: Yes, just a pound of sugar, if you don't mind.

A: What time is it?
B: It's quarter to four.
A: Then I must go to the laundry.
B: Will you be passing the chemist's on your way?
A: Yes, I will. Do you need anything?
B: Yes, just a packet of aspirins, if you don't mind.

PRACTICE

A: What's the time? // What time is it?
B: It's . . . 6.
A: Then I must go to the . . . 7.
B: Will you be passing the . . . 7 on your way?
A: Yes, I will. Do you need anything?
B: Yes, just a(an) . . . 5, if you don't mind.

6	7	5
ten o'clock	paper shop	evening paper
eleven o'clock	greengrocer's	dozen oranges
ten to nine	baker's	loaf of bread
ten past nine	outfitter's	yard of lace
	jeweller's	packet of pins
	builder's	watch strap
	bank	little cement
	stores	new cheque book
	post-office	half a pound of butter
	sweet shop	book of stamps
		few bars of chocolate

19

I'll be seeing you on Tuesday then

A: I'll be seeing you on Tuesday then.
B: I'm afraid not. I shan't be coming here on Tuesday.
A: But I must give you back your book.
B: That's all right. You'll be rehearsing the play with Bill on Tuesday, won't you? Give it to him then.

A: I'll be seeing you on Tuesday then.
B: I'm afraid not. I shan't be coming here on Tuesday.
A: But I must give you back your book.
B: That's all right. You'll be going to church with Mary on Sunday, won't you? Give it to her then.

... rehearsing the play with Bill.

PRACTICE

A: I'll be seeing you on Tuesday then.
B: I'm afraid not. I shan't be coming here on Tuesday.
A: But I must give you back your book.
B: That's all right. You'll be ... 1 + ing X on ... 6, won't you? Give it to him/her then.

1 + ing	6
having lunch with tea	Monday
visiting	Wednesday
seeing	Thursday
going to the pictures with see	Friday
calling on	Saturday
doing some work with	
shopping with	
attending the meeting with	

20

It's often very hot in summer *

A: What country are you from?
B: From India.
A: What's the climate like there?
B: I like it, but it's often very hot in summer.

A: What country are you from?
B: From New Zealand.
A: What's the climate like there?
B: I like it, but it's sometimes very windy in winter.

PRACTICE

A: What country are you from?
B: From . . . 5.
A: What's the climate like there?
B: I like it, but it's . . . 8 very . . . 4 in . . . 6.

5	**8**	**4**	**6**
Pakistan	almost always	cold	spring
Britain	occasionally	wet	autumn
Sweden	sometimes	sultry	
Norway	seldom	stormy	
Queensland	hardly ever	cloudy	
Brazil	frequently	pleasant	
Canada			

I sometimes give her a bunch of flowers

A: What do you usually give your mother for her birthday?
B: I sometimes give her a bunch of flowers, and sometimes a box of chocolates.
A: I always give my mother a book.
B: Oh, I never give books as birthday presents.

A: What do you usually give your uncle for his birthday?
B: I often give him a pipe, and sometimes tobacco.
A: I always give my uncle socks.
B: Oh, I hardly ever give socks as birthday presents.

I often give him a pipe.

PRACTICE

A: What do you usually give your . . . 5 for his/her birthday?
B: I . . . 8 give him/her . . . 5a, and . . , 8 . . . 5a.
A: I always give my 5 . . . 5a.
B: Oh, I never/hardly ever give . . . 5a as a birthday present.

5	8	5a
father	occasionally = *not often*	brooch
aunt	frequently / *often*	necklace
brother	generally / *usually*	wallet
sister	almost always	cheque
nephew	*sometimes*	pen
niece	*hardly ever /*	knife
son	*rarely*	doll
daughter		mechanical toy
cousin	*never*	money
grandmother		cosmetics
grandfather		things for the garden
	always	jewellery
	usually	sweets
	frequently / often	
	sometimes	
	not often	
	hardly ever / rarely	
	never	

22

It hardly ever rains

A: Have you ever been to Scotland?
B: I've only been there once, but I've often been to Wales.
A: I've never been to Wales. Is it pleasant there?
B: Oh, very pleasant, but it frequently rains in summer.

A: Have you ever been to Egypt?
B: I've only been there once, but I've often been to the Lebanon.
A: I've never been to the Lebanon. It is pleasant there?
B: Oh, very pleasant, but it hardly ever rains in summer.

Have you ever been to Egypt?

PRACTICE

A: Have you ever been to . . . 7?
B: I've only been there once, but I've often been to . . . 7.
A: I've never been to . . . 7. Is it pleasant there?
B: Oh, very pleasant, but it . . . 8 rains in . . . 6.

7	8	6
Italy	sometimes	winter
France	always	spring
Morocco	often	autumn
Spain	occasionally	
Portugal	never	
Norway		
Denmark		
Canada		
Mexico		

She has seldom done any housework

A: Jim is going to become a professional footballer.
B: Is he really?
A: Yes, he is, though he has never played in the school team.
B: How extraordinary!

A: Jane is going to become a nurse.
B: Is she really?
A: Yes, she is, though she has seldom done any housework.
B: How strange!

PRACTICE

A: **X** is going to . . . **1**.
B: Is he/she really?
A: Yes, he/she is, though he/she has . . . **3**.
B: How strange/extraordinary!

1

go on the stage
   to the university
act in films
take up chemistry
   flying
become a film star
buy a car
join the army

3

always disliked	the theatre
	cinema
	explosives
	heights
	discipline
often	sneered at acting
sometimes	motoring
occasionally	
hardly ever	learned anything by heart
	been studious

He has never been away from home

A: I have a new friend. His name is Alfred.
B: So I've heard. Tell me about him.
A: He has never been away from home.
B: I can hardly believe it!

A: I have a new colleague. Her name is Joan.
B: So I've heard. Tell me about her.
A: She has frequently won races.
B: How interesting!

She has frequently won races.

PRACTICE

A: I have a new friend/colleague. His/Her name is **X**.
B: Tell me about him/her.
A: He/She has **. . . 3**.
B: How interesting. // I can hardly believe it!

3

often been in the news
twice swum the Channel
occasionally appeared on TV
once been in prison
always voted Conservative
hardly ever read a newspaper
never been in a motor car
always lived in a caravan

The Browns and the Greens

A : We've got visitors coming to tea today.
B : What visitors?
A : The Browns and the Greens.
B : I expect they'll be bringing their children along.

A : We've got visitors coming to lunch today.
B : What visitors?
A : The Johnsons and the Whites.
B : I expect they'll be bringing their dogs along.

PRACTICE

A : We've got visitors coming to tea / lunch / dinner today.
B : What visitors?
A : The Xs and the Ys.
B : I expect they'll be bringing their . . . 5 along.

5

pets
guests
slides
records
photograph album

A Mr Green called

A: A Mr Green called when you were out.
B: A Mr Green? Was he short and fat?
A: Yes, he was.
B: Then it was Mr Robert Green?
A: *The* Robert Green?
B: Yes. Robert Green the famous atomic scientist.

A: A Miss Wilson called when you were out.
B: A Miss Wilson? Was she large and jolly?
A: Yes, she was.
B: Then it was Miss Ada Wilson.
A: *The* Ada Wilson?
B: Yes. Ada Wilson the well-known novelist.

... the famous scientist.

PRACTICE

A: A Mr/Mrs/Miss **X** called when you were out.
B: A Mr/Mrs/Miss **X**? Was he/she . . . **4** and . . . **4**?
A: Yes, he/she was.
B: Then it was **XY**.
A: *The* **XY**?
B: Yes. **XY** the famous/well known . . . **5**.

4		5	
tall	freckled	racing motorist	boxer
thin	short-sighted	test pilot	swimmer
red-faced	well dressed	poet	judge
pale	handsome	screen star	member of parliament
dark	well built	pop singer	actor/actress
fair	pretty	preacher	jockey
in glasses			

Modern art and the art of Michelangelo †

A: Bill is writing a book.
B: What is it about?
A: About economics.
B: How interesting!

A: Iris is writing a book.
B: What is it about?
A: About the economics of publishing.
B: How interesting!

PRACTICE

A: **X** is writing a book.
B: What is it about?
A: About . . . **5 (a** or **b)**.
B: How interesting!

5a	5b
modern art	the art of Michelangelo
classical music	music of Chopin
modern life	life of Nelson
contemporary society	society of Ancient Greece
English literature	English literature of the Thirties
American poetry	poetry of Milton
philosophy	philosophy of Shakespeare
old furniture	furniture of Roman Britain
ancient history	history of France
Egypt	Egypt of the Pharaohs

† Both dialogues on this page are recorded on the accompanying tape.

The application of new methods in industry †

A: I'm taking part in a debate today.
B: What is it about?
A: About the application of new methods in industry.
B: I didn't know you were interested in such problems.

A: I'm taking part in a debate today.
B: What is it about?
A: About new methods in industry.
B: I didn't realize you were interested in such problems.

PRACTICE

A: I'm taking part in a debate today.
B: What is it about?
A: About . . . **5 (a** or **b).**
B: I didn't know/realize you were interested in such problems.

5a	5b
the uses of rubber in industry	rubber
synthetic fibres	synthetic fibres
production of rubber tyres	rubber tyres
synthetic rubber	production in the rubber industry
tyres	industrial organization
organization of production	coal
coal ⎫	iron
iron ⎪ industry	copper
copper ⎬	steel
steel ⎭	manufacture and marketing
manufacture of refrigerators	

† Neither of the dialogues on this page is recorded on the accompanying tape.

The necessity for a sense of humour

A: I've been reading a very interesting book this week.
B: What is it about?
A: About the necessity for a sense of humour.
B: It doesn't sound very interesting to me.

A: I've been reading a very interesting book this week.
B: What is it about?
A: About the rise in the cost of living.
B: It doesn't sound very interesting to me.

. . . *unemployment in Ruritania.*

PRACTICE

A: I've been reading a very interesting book this week.
B: What is it about?
A: About . . . 5.
B: It doesn't sound very interesting to me.

5

the need for a better understanding among people
problem of unemployment
        the present unemployment in Ruritania
causes of the increase of heart trouble among clerical workers
publicity given to film stars
development of the motor industry in Italy
availability of information about the weather
advice given to statesmen by economic experts
lack of medical services in country districts

If it's a nice day tomorrow

A: If it's a nice day tomorrow, I'll go and play tennis.
B: And if it isn't nice?
A: If it isn't nice, I'll stay at home and study English.
B: So shall I.

A: If it's a nice day tomorrow, I'll work in the garden.
B: And if it isn't nice?
A: If it isn't nice, I'll stay indoors and watch television.
B: So shall I.

PRACTICE

A: If it's a nice day tomorrow, I'll . . . **1**.
B: And if it isn't nice?
A: If it isn't nice, I'll . . . **1a**.
B: So shall I.

1

take my wife for a drive
  family for a picnic
do some sailing
  skiing
  gardening
go to the football match
  on the river
  fishing
  swimming
prune the roses
have a walk in the woods

1a

clean the car
arrange my stamps
play the gramophone
  chess
listen to some records
read a novel
have a quiet day
work in the greenhouse
  on my book

What will you do if it's raining?

A: I'm going on an excursion tomorrow.
B: But what will you do if it's raining?
A: If it's raining, I'll stay under cover.
B: I think you'll have to!

A: I'm going on an excursion tomorrow.
B: But what will you do if it turns wet?
A: If it turns wet, I'll go to the pictures instead.
B: I think you'll have to!

I'll go just the same.

PRACTICE

A: I'm going on an excursion tomorrow.
B: But what will you do if it . . . **1 + s**?
A: If it . . . **1 + s**, I'll . . . **1**.
B: I think you'll have to!

1 + s

turns windy
    stormy
snows
's very hot
    cold
    foggy
  thundery
  drizzling
blows a gale
sets in wet

1

come home again
take an umbrella
    a sunshade
put off the excursion
go swimming at the baths
cancel the outing
go just the same

32

. . . If he doesn't take more care

A: Bill is a very careless driver.
B: Yes, I'm afraid so.
A: He may cause an accident if he doesn't take more care.
B: That's what I'm afraid of.

A: Elsie is a very careless driver.
B: Yes, I'm afraid so.
A: She may cause an accident if she doesn't watch the road.
B: That's what I'm afraid of.

PRACTICE

A: **X** is a very careless driver.
B: Yes, I'm afraid so.
A: He/She may cause an accident if he/she . . . **1 + s.**
B: That's what I'm afraid of.

1 + s.

doesn't give up beer
   observe the traffic rules
   stop talking so much
   learn the Highway Code
   obey the road signs
   give the proper signals
goes on driving so fast
always insists on overtaking

I shall if it's not too wet *

A : Are you going to play football tomorrow?
B : I will if I'm not too tired.
A : But if you are tired?
B : Then I'll go to bed instead.

A : Are you going to have a picnic tomorrow?
B : I shall if it's not too wet.
A : But if it is wet?
B : Then I'll stay indoors instead.

PRACTICE

A : Are you going to . . . **1** tomorrow?
B : I will/shall if I'm/it's not too . . **.4**.
A : But if you are/it is . . . **4**?
B : Then I'll . . . **1a** instead.

1	4	1a
play golf	busy	read a book
cards	sleepy	watch TV
tennis	lazy	have a rest
go to the theatre	stormy	do some sewing
meeting	rainy	my work
finish that game of chess	cold	play with the children
your knitting		
do some baking		
your homework		
work in the garden		
see the new film		

I will if I get a rise

A: Will you go abroad for your holidays next summer?
B: Yes, I will, if I get a rise this year.
A: Are you expecting one?
B: Yes, I am, and I shall be very disappointed if I don't get it.

A: Will you enter for the championship next year?
B: Yes, I will, if I get a prize this year.
A: Are you expecting one?
B: Yes, I am, and I shall be very disappointed if I don't get it.

. . . a good price for cows.

PRACTICE

A: Will you . . . **1** next summer/year?
B: Yes, I will, if I get . . . **5** this year.
A: Are you expecting one?
B: Yes, I am, and I shall be very disappointed if I don't get it.

1

grow wheat on your farm
    beans in your garden
go fishing for your holiday
write another book
hatch any chickens
gather mushrooms
sell any cattle

5

a good crop
  big catch
  good sale for my last one
have a good hatch
a lot
  good price for cows

What will you do if he can't come?*

A: I'm going to propose to Jill tomorrow.
B: What will you do if she turns you down?
A: If she turns me down, I'll probably go abroad.

A: I'm going to the theatre with Tom tomorrow.
B: What will you do if he can't come?
A: If he can't come, I'll probably go by myself.

PRACTICE

A: I'm going to . . . **1** tomorrow.
B: What will you do if he/she . . . **1+s**?
A: If he/she . . . **1+s**, I'll probably . . . **1a**.

1	**1+s**	**1a**
play chess with **X**	refuses	read a book
practise music with **X**	isn't in the mood	watch TV
take **X** to a dance	doesn't turn up	find someone else
concert	can't get home in time	go for a walk instead
the pictures	changes his/her mind	
theatre		
play tennis with **X**		
go for a walk with **X**		

If you move to London, you'll not see your parents

A: I don't know whether to move to London or not.
B: If you move to London, you'll not see your parents so often.
A: But if I don't, I'll not get such a good job.
B: I don't know about that.

A: I don't know whether to learn to ride or not.
B: If you learn to ride, you'll be badly out of pocket.
A: But if I don't, I'll miss a lot of fun.
B: That's true.

. . . start learning Chinese.

PRACTICE

A: I don't know whether to . . . **1** or not.
B: If you . . . **1**, you'll . . . **1a**.
A: But if I don't, I'll . . . **1b**.
B: That's true. // I don't know about that.

1	**1a**	**1b**
move to town	lose your freedom	be rather miserable
Edinburgh	find it very noisy	feel lonely
Glasgow	have to pay for it	have too much
get married	be worrying all the time	walking to do
start learning Chinese	get bored with it	waste a lot of time
give up smoking	save a lot of money	get lazy
buy a car	feel very well	have no regular job
scooter	dislike the discipline	feel happier
house		
join the Army		
Navy		
Air Force		

Let's start when the postman's been

A: May I help you with the housework?
B: You may if you like, but you don't have to.
A: If I don't help you, I shall feel rather lazy.
B: Then let's start when the postman's been.

A: May I help you with the garden?
B: You may if you like, but you don't have to.
A: If I don't help you, I shan't feel happy.
B: Then let's start when we've finished breakfast.

PRACTICE

A: May I help you with . . . 5?
B: You may if you like, but you don't have to.
A: If I don't help you, I shall feel rather lazy//shan't feel happy.
B: Then let's start when . . . 9.

5	9
the cooking	the clock strikes nine
washing	children go to school
digging	have gone to school
painting	grass has dried
decorating	rain stops
cleaning	sun comes out
making the beds	Father comes home
fires	lunch
planting the potatoes	dinner } is finished
milking the cows	
cutting the grass	

She will when she changes her hair style*

A: Do you think Jack will ever get down to work?
B: I think he will when he gets more reliable.
A: But when will he do that?
B: When he leaves home.

A: Do you think Susan will ever look smart?
B: I think she will when she changes her hair style.
A: But when will she do that?
B: When she gets older.

PRACTICE

A: Do you think **X** will ever . . . **1**?
B: I think he/she will when he/she . . . **1+s**.
A: But when will he/she do that?
B: When he/she . . . **1+S**

When she gets older.

1

settle down
become more serious
take me to the pictures
pass his/her exams
come to see us

1+s

gets more time
money
married
changes his/her company
starts work
leaves school
grows more serious

1+S
starts earning
's eighteen
moves into lodgings
has to pay for his/her board and lodgings
joins the Army/Navy/Air Force

Stay here till I come back

A : How long must I stay?
B : Stay here till I come back.
A : But how long will that be?
B : I shan't return till it's dark.

A : How long should I wait?
B : Wait here till your father comes back.
A : But how long will that be?
B : He won't return till he has milked the cows.

PRACTICE

A : How long must/should I wait/stay?
B : Wait/Stay here till **X** come(s) back.
A : But how long will that be?
B : I shan't,   return till . . . **9**.
   He/She won't

9

the moon rises
   rain has stopped
   street lights come on
his/her work is finished
you hear the bus come
   have finished your homework
the children are in bed
night comes on

She's waiting until she can afford it

A: Why isn't Peggy going on holiday?
B: She's waiting until she can afford it.
A: How long will that be?
B: Several months, I expect.

A: Why isn't David getting married?
B: He's waiting until he gets a house.
A: How long will that be?
B: Several months, I expect.

PRACTICE

A: Why isn't **X** . . . **1 + ing**?
B: He/She's waiting until he/she . . . **1 + s**.
A: How long will that be?
B: Several months, I expect.

. . . until he gets a house.

1 + ing

playing football
   in the team
coming to visit us
planting up the garden
writing another book
starting his/her own business
   in practice
going to America

1 + s

is fit again
get's the doctor's permission
gets his/her new bicycle
had less work at the office
gets the last one published
is qualified
finds a partner
had his/her passport

41

. . . *Unless he earns more*

A: When's Tom going to buy a scooter?
B: He won't buy a scooter unless he gets a rise in wages.
A: But if he doesn't?
B: Then he'll buy a bicycle.

A: When's Jane going to start work?
B: She won't start work unless she gets rid of her asthma.
A: But if she doesn't?
B: Then she'll stay at home.

PRACTICE

A: When's **X** going to . . . **1**?
B: He/She won't . . . **1** unless he/she . . . **1 + s**.
A: But if he/she doesn't?
B: Then he/she'll . . . **1a**.

1	**1 + s**	**1a**
buy a house	inherits a legacy	live in a flat
learn to drive	buys a car	use the bus
do the garden	gives up football golf	let Mother do it
go abroad for a holiday	sells his /her car	take his/her holiday at home
for a walk	gets a letter from **X**	sit indoors all day
get up	feels better	stay in bed all day

... *Before he emigrates*

A: My brother is going to emigrate to Canada soon.
B: He ought to get qualified before he emigrates.
A: But he has done so.
B: Sorry, I didn't know.

A: My sister is going to get married soon.
B: She ought to take her degree before she gets married.
A: But she has done so.
B: Sorry, I didn't know.

... *emigrate to Canada.*

PRACTICE

A: **X** is going to . . . **1** soon.
B: He/She ought to . . . **1a** before he/she . . . **1+s**.
A: But he/she has done so.
B: Sorry, I didn't know.

1	1a	1+s
buy a house	pay for his/her car	buys a house
car	motor bike	buys a car
open a shop	save some money	opens a shop
mow the lawn	clip the hedge	mows the lawn
play chess	take the dog out	plays chess
sell his/her bicycle	ask Father's permission	sells his/her bike
join the Army	finish school	joins the Army

She had learned to dance

A: Kate was very clever as a child.
B: Was she really?
A: Oh, yes. By the time she was three she had learned to dance.
B: How remarkable!

A: Bob was very clever as a child.
B: Was he really?
A: Oh, yes. By the time he was five he had mastered the violin.
B: How remarkable!

. . . mastered the violin.

PRACTICE

A: X was very clever as a child.
B: Was he/she really?
A: Oh, yes. By the time he/she was . . . **4** he/she had . . . **3**.
B: How remarkable!

4	**3**
four	learned to swim
six	type
seven	read Latin
eight	read and write
nine	written a book
ten	three books
	a poem
	composed a song
	symphony
	broken records at swimming
	running
	won a skating contest
	had a painting on exhibition
	played in a band
	an orchestra

How long had he been a teacher?

A: How long have you known Jim Black?
B: For six years. I met him at my uncle's six years ago.
A: How long had he been a teacher at that time?
B: For about two years.

A: How long have you known Kitty Smith?
B: For many years. I met her at my uncle's many years ago.
A: How long had she been a tennis player then?
B: For about three years.

PRACTICE

A: How long have you known **X**?
B: For ... **6**. I met him/her at my uncle's ... **6** ago.
A: How long had he/she ... **3** at that time?/then?
B: For about ... **6**.

6	**3**
one year	known your uncle
four years	sister
five	French
seven	been married
eight	a student
nine	gambler
	football player
	had a car
	scooter
	lived in your town
	village
	been a well-known actor/actress
	film star
	novelist

He had got married

A : I hear you had a telephone call from Edward yesterday.
B : Yes, I did. He phoned to tell me that he had got married.
A : What else did he say.
B : He said he was going to Florida.

A : I hear you had a telephone call from Vera yesterday.
B : Yes, I did. She phoned to tell me that she had decided to emigrate.
A : What else did she say?
B : She said she was going to fly to Australia.

. . . hurt in an accident.

PRACTICE

A : I hear you had a telephone call from **X** yesterday.
B : Yes, I did. He/She phoned to tell me that he/she had **. . . 3**.
A : What else did he/she say?
B : He/She said he/she was going to **. . . 1**.

3

got his/her degree
    engaged
    promotion

changed his/her job
bought a house
    car
moved to Birmingham
been hurt in an accident

1

take a teaching post
get married soon
buy a new house
    car
start working for his/her father
resign from our club
sell his/her motorcycle
work in a factory
be away from work for a week

The front wheel is buckled

A: What's the matter?
B: I've just fallen off my bicycle.
A: Oh dear! Is anything broken?
B: I'm afraid the front wheel is buckled.

A: What's the matter?
B: I've just fallen off my bicycle.
A: Oh dear! Is anything broken?
B: No, but I'm afraid my wrist is sprained.

PRACTICE

A: What's the matter?
B: I've just fallen off my bicycle.
A: Oh dear! Is anything broken?
B: (No, but) I'm afraid . . . 9.

9

the tyre is punctured
    handle-bars are twisted
    pedals are bent
my hand/knee is cut
    leg is bruised
    suit is spoiled
    hat is lost
    satchel is ruined
    glasses are smashed
    watch is broken

I want to be chosen

A: Are you going to the meeting tonight?
B: Yes, I think so.
A: Why?
B: Because I want to be chosen for the committee.

A: Are you going to the theatre tonight?
B: Yes, I think so.
A: Why?
B: Because I want to be amused.

PRACTICE

A: Are you going . . . **7** tonight?
B: Yes, I think so.
A: Why?
B: Because I want to be . . . **3**.

. . . my new bathing costume.

7
to the team meeting
    dancing lesson
    club
    conference
for a swim
with **X** to the party

3
made captain
taught to dance
selected for the team
sent to London
seen in my new bathing costume
given a lift

48

It was announced yesterday

A: What's the news?
B: Michael is going to be sent to America to do research work.
A: When did you hear that?
B: It was announced yesterday.

A: What's the news?
B: My uncle is going to be promoted.
A: When did you hear that?
B: It was published yesterday.

PRACTICE

A: What's the news?
B: **X** is going to be **. . . 3**.
A: When did you hear that?
B: It was **. . . 3a** yesterday.

3

made a director
given a presentation
granted a bonus
awarded the Nobel prize
nominated for Parliament
summoned for dangerous driving
elected captain
retired on pension

3a

generally known
stated
given out on the radio
mentioned to me
reported in the papers
strongly rumoured

He'll be given a scholarship

A: I envy Bill.
B: Why?
A: Because he'll be given a scholarship next year.
B: Well, he deserves it.

A: I don't envy Elsie.
B: Why?
A: Because she'll be dismissed next week.
B: Well, she deserves it.

PRACTICE

A: I (don't) envy **X**.
B: Why?
A: Because he/she'll be ... **3** next year/week.
B: Well, he/she deserves it

... presented to the Queen.

3

given a grant
      present
      notice
chosen for the touring team
made a director
passed over for promotion
promoted
presented to the Queen
invited to the ball
elected captain of the team

He's been turned down*

A: I've had a letter from my brother.
B: How's he getting on?
A: He's been turned down by the Navy.
B: Poor fellow!

A: I've had a letter from my sister.
B: How's she getting on?
A: She's been accepted for college.
B: I'm so glad.

PRACTICE

A: I've had a letter from my brother/sister.
B: How's he/she getting on?
A: He's/She's been . . . 3.
B: Poor fellow/girl! // I'm so glad.

3

promoted captain
placed in charge
offered a directorship
       partnership
made headmaster/headmistress
injured in an accident
taken to hospital
declared bankrupt
flooded out at home
ruined by bad crops
      the poor harvest
awarded a scholarship

My watch has been stolen

A: I must call the police.
B: Why?
A: Because my watch has been stolen.
B: I *am* sorry. I hope it'll soon be recovered.

A: I must call the police.
B: Why?
A: Because my cash-box has been stolen.
B: I *am* sorry. I hope it'll soon be found.

PRACTICE

A: I must call the police.
B: Why?
A: Because my **. . . 5** has been stolen.
B: I *am* sorry. I hope it'll soon be found/recovered.

5

wallet
car
scooter
passport
cheque book
ring
luggage
brief case
purse
necklace

A new school is being built

A: Why do you look so worried?

B: Because a new school is being built near my house.

A: But why are you upset about that?

B: Because I don't like noise.

A: Why do you look so worried?

B: Because a new public house is being opened near my house.

A: But why are you upset about that?

B: Because I don't like crowds.

I don't like noise.

PRACTICE

A: Why do you look so worried?

B: Because a new ... 5 is being built/opened near my house.

A: But why are you upset about that?

B: Because I don't like ... ... 5a.

5	5a
hospital	factory noises
factory	smells
power station	smoke
gasworks	the smell of petrol
railway station	traffic
service station	too many people about
football stadium	
supermarket	

It's being widely advertised

A: Fred has invented a new typewriter.
B: Has he really?
A: Yes, he has. It's being widely advertised.
B: How interesting!

A: My aunt has invented a new game of cards.
B: Has she really?
A: Yes, she has. It's being played a lot in our town.
B: How interesting!

PRACTICE

A: X has invented a new . . . 5.
B: Has he/she really?
A: Yes, he/she has. It's being . . . 3.
B: How interesting!

5	3
washing machine	used a lot
dance	danced in all the smart clubs
drink	asked for everywhere
motor engine	patented right away
toy	supplied by all the toy shops
kitchen gadget	sold at all the big shops
fountain pen	offered by all the stationers
material	produced by a leading firm

I found my car had been stolen

A: Why didn't you come to
the English lesson yesterday?
B: Because I had to go to the
police.
A: What for?
B: When I got home I found
my car had been stolen.

A: Why didn't you come to
the club yesterday?
B: Because I had to go to the
police.
A: What for?
B: When I got home I found
my house had been bur-
gled.

. . . my dog had been stolen.

PRACTICE

A: Why didn't you come to the . . . 5 yesterday?
B: Because I had to go to the police.
A: What for?
B: When I got home I found . . . 9.

5
party
tennis match
pictures
reunion
meeting
committee meeting
dance

9
my house had been broken into
    flat
    room
    garage
my scooter had been stolen
    furniture
    jewels
    books
    revolver
    dog
    TV set
    passport
a bomb had been placed under my bed
all my whisky had been drunk
    my food had been eaten
my orchard had been robbed

55

He's afraid of being punished

A: Joe doesn't want to go to school.
B: Why not?
A: Because he's afraid of being given too much homework.
B: How silly!

A: My sister doesn't want to go to school.
B: Why not?
A: Because she's afraid of being made to work too hard.
B: How silly!

PRACTICE

A: **X** doesn't want to go to school.
B: Why not?
A: Because he's/she's afraid of being **. . . 3**.
B: How silly!

3

asked too many questions
corrected
given bad marks
examined
caned
punished
beaten by the other children
disciplined
put in uniform
made to wear a cap/hat

Jack mustn't be told

A: Let's go to a concert, shall
we?
B: Splendid, but Jack mustn't
be told about it.
A: Why not?
B: Because he'd be jealous.

A: Let's take painting lessons,
shall we?
B: Splendid, but Kate mustn't
be told about it.
A: Why not?
B: Because she'd stop us.

Let's join the Boy Scouts . . .

PRACTICE

A: Let's . . . **1**, shall we?
B: Splendid, but **X** mustn't be
told about it.
A: Why not?
B: Because he'd/she'd . . .
1a.

1

go swimming
   for a picnic
stay out late
let the dog loose
pick some apples
     plums
eat all the chocolates
join the Boy Scouts//Girl Guides

1a

be angry with us
   very upset
   unhappy
stop our pocket money
send us to bed
make a scene
    row
complain
hate being left out

He's said to be very exacting

A : We're going to have a new teacher.
B : Do you know anything about him?
A : Yes. His name is John Brown. He's said to be very exacting.
B : I hope we'll like him all the same.

A : We're going to have a new mistress.
B : Do you know anything about her?
A : Yes. Her name is Miss White. She's said to be very strict.
B : I hope we'll like her all the same.

PRACTICE

A : We're going to have a new . . . **5**.
B : Do you know anything about him/her?
A : Yes. He's/She's said to be very . . . **4**.
B : I hope we'll like him/her all the same.

5	**4**
boss	punctual
secretary	severe
music master/mistress	serious
inspector	stern
police constable	arrogant
headmaster/headmistress	unsociable
	pompous

It's said to be one of the most beautiful places

A: Did you visit Stratford during your stay in Britain?
B: We were supposed to, but we didn't.
A: What a pity!
B: I know, it's said to be one of the most beautiful places in Britain.

A: Did you see the Tower of London during your stay in Britain?
B: We were supposed to, but we didn't.
A: What a pity!
B: I know, it's thought to be one of the best sights of London.

Did you see the Tower of London . . .

PRACTICE

A: Did you visit . . . **5** during your stay in Britain?
B: We were supposed to, but we didn't.
A: What a pity!
B: I know, it's . . . **3** one of the ⎱ most beautiful places in Britain.
⎰ best sights of London.

5

the Peak District
   Lake District
   Trossachs
Snowdonia
Dartmoor
Exmoor
the Cornish coast
Windsor Castle
Buckingham Palace
Kew Gardens
St Paul's Cathedral
Westminster Abbey

3

believed to be
considered as
regarded as
described as
supposed to be
known to be

I don't want to be run over*

A: I'm not going to the concert.
B: But you are expected to.
A: I know, but I don't want to be bored to death.
B: You needn't be afraid of that.

A: I'm not going to the motor racing.
B: But you are expected to.
A: I know, but I don't want to be run over.
B: You needn't be afraid of that.

PRACTICE

A: I'm not going to . . . 5.
B: But you are expected to.
A: I know, but I don't want to be . . . 3.
B: You needn't be afraid of that.

5	3
the races	trampled to death
cinema	suffocated
swimming bath	laughed at
dentist's	tortured
doctor's	frightened
conference	made to speak
church	frozen to death
London	hurt in an accident

Bill said he would be a doctor

A: On leaving school Bill said he would be a doctor.
B: When was that?
A: Six years ago.
B: Has he carried out his plan?
A: No, he hasn't. He's become a teacher.

A: On leaving school Miss Jones said she would be a nurse.
B: When was that?
A: Six years ago.
B: Has she carried out her plan?
A: No, she hasn't. She's become a housewife.

PRACTICE

A: On leaving school **X** said he/she would be a(an) **. . . 5**.
B: When was that?
A: Six years ago.
B: Has he/she carried out his/her plan?
A: No, he/she hasn't. He's/She's become a(an) **. . . 5**.

5

economist	policewoman
accountant	lawyer
university lecturer	vet
pilot	civil servant
airman	taxi-driver
air hostess	racing motorist
sailor	professional cyclist
soldier	film star
policeman	photographer

*She said she was going to leave home**

A : I met Jim last week. We
had a chat.
B : What did you talk about?
A : He said he would prob-
ably emigrate to Australia.
B : I wonder if he will.

A : I met Sally last week. We
had a chat.
B : What did you talk about?
A : She said she was going to
leave home.
B : I wonder if she will.

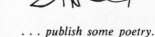

. . . publish some poetry.

PRACTICE

A : I met **X** last week. We
had a chat.
B : What did you talk about?
A : He/She said he/she would
probably//was going to
. . . 1.
B : I wonder if he/she will.

1

turn professional
change his/her job
throw up his/her career
join the Army
        Navy
        Air Force
sell his/her house
            collection of stamps
buy a farm
write a novel
publish some poetry

If I had a lot of money . . .

A : If I had a lot of money, I'd go on a trip round the world.
B : And if I had a lot of money, I'd buy a big house.
A : And what would Mary do if she had a lot of money?
B : Oh, she'd probably give most of it away.

A : If I had a lot of time, I'd go for a long walking tour.
B : And if I had a lot of time, I'd make the garden very attractive.
A : And what would Bill do if he had a lot of time?
B : Oh, he'd probably play golf every day.

PRACTICE

A : If I had a lot of money/time, I'd . . . 1.
B : And if I had a lot of money/time, I'd . . . 1.
A : And what would **X** do if he/she had a lot of money/time?
B : Oh, he'd/she'd probably . . . 1.

1

buy a large car
    racehorse
    farm
    an estate
visit Monte Carlo
go on a luxury cruise
    climbing in the Himalayas
    to Canada
    South America
    Australia
enlarge the business

have a house in the country
    long holiday
    complete rest
    dozens of new suits/dresses
take music lessons
learn to play golf
    bridge
    billiards
    Greek
    Arabic
write a book

. . . if you had a chance to?

A: Would you go in for motor racing if you had a chance to?
B: Yes, I would.
A: So would I.
B: It would be very exciting, I expect.

A: Would you go to the moon if you had a chance to?
B: No, I wouldn't.
A: Neither would I.
B: It would be very dangerous, I expect.

. . . a deep sea diver.

PRACTICE

A: Would you **1** if you had a chance to?
B: Yes, I would. // No, I wouldn't.
A: So would I. // Neither would I.
B: It would be very . . . **4**, I expect.

1

be a ballet dancer
    mountaineer
    racing cyclist
    deep sea diver
  an actor/actress
learn to ski
    ski-jump
    gliding
play tennis
    hockey
fly an aeroplane
go in for long distance running
    horse-riding

4

amusing
thrilling
frightening
enthralling
tiring
nerve-wracking
boring
demanding

. . . if you won a lot of money?

A: What would you do if you won a lot of money?
B: I'd buy a big house in the country.
A: And when you had done that?
B: I'd retire and live there.

A: What would you do if you inherited a fortune?
B: I'd go for a cruise round the world.
A: And when you had done that?
B: I'd buy a yacht of my own.

PRACTICE

A: What would you do if you . . . 2?
B: I'd . . . 1.
A: And when you had done that?
B: I'd . . . 1.

2	1
became rich	open a home for orphans
	endow a hospital
owned a large estate	breed pedigree horses
	open a racing stable
had to join the army	enlist as a paratrooper
	volunteer for overseas service
were a good athlete	try to be chosen for the Olympic Games
	become a sports writer
lived in America	visit California
	see the great National park
met a lion	climb a tree
	call for help
got lost in the desert	take my directions from the sun
	be still in the heat of the day

65

What would you do if you won the lottery?

A: What would you do if you won the lottery this week?
B: I'd buy a car.
A: Wouldn't it be more in-interesting to go round the world?
B: No, I don't think it would.

A: What would you do if you won the lottery this week?
B: I'd buy a new house.
A: Wouldn't it be more inter-esting to buy a yacht?
B: Yes, perhaps it would.

. . . get some pedigree cats.

PRACTICE

A: What would you do if you won the lottery this week?
B: I'd . . . **1**.
A: Wouldn't it be more in-teresting to . . . **1a**?
B: Yes, perhaps it would.//
No, I don't think it would.

1

buy a good gun
    new wardrobe
invest in a farm
live in a hotel
get a business
engage a servant
order some pedigree dogs

1a

buy a fishing rod
    new TV set
have a long holiday
live in a luxury flat
buy a caravan
learn a new trade
hire a driver
get some pedigree cats

I'd like to work as an interpreter*

A: What would you do if you changed your job?
B: I'd like to work as a foreign trade expert.
A: Why would you choose that?
B: Because I'd be able to travel a lot.

A: What would you do if you changed your job?
B: I'd like to work as an interpreter.
A: Why would you choose that?
B: Because I'd be able to meet interesting people.

PRACTICE

A: What would you do if you changed your job?
B: I'd like to work as a(an) . . . **5**.
A: Why would you choose that?
B: Because I'd be able to . . . **1**.

5	1
racing motorist	live dangerously
airline pilot	see the world
university teacher	train good minds
diplomat	study politics
politician	get real power
surgeon	relieve pain
nurse	take care of people
architect	design beautiful buildings
sailor	visit many countries

Taking the dog for a run

A: Where have you been?
B: I've been for a walk, taking the dog for a run.
A: And I've been busy, getting tea ready.
B: I hope I'm not late for tea.

A: Where have you been?
B: I've been riding my bicycle, getting some exercise.
A: And I've been busy, getting tea ready.
B: I hope I'm not late for tea.

. . . taking the dog for a run.

PRACTICE

A: Where have you been?
B: I've been . . . **1 + ing.**
A: And I've been busy, getting tea ready.
B: I hope I'm not late for tea.

1 + ing

working in the garden, cutting the hedge
mowing the lawn
planting potatoes
cabbages
beans
carrots
garage, mending the car
washing the car
shed, potting plants
sitting on the verandah, shelling peas
idling on the beach, reading a book

Could you show me the way to the post office, please?

A: Could you show me the way to the post office, please?

B: Certainly. Take the second road on the left, and it's a little way down on the right.

A: Thank you very much.

A: Could you tell me how to get to the station, please?

B: Certainly. Take the first road on the right, and it's a little way down on the left.

A: Thank you very much.

. . . the way to a hospital.

PRACTICE

A: Could you show me the way to//tell me how to get to . . . 5, please?

B: Certainly. Take the . . . 4 road on the left/right and it's a little way down on the right/left.

A: Thank you very much.

5	4
the church	third
nearest pillar box	fourth
garage	fifth
bridge	sixth
High Street	next
public library	
football ground	
a hospital	
park	
hotel	

Could you come tomorrow?

A: I'd like to have a long chat with you.
B: Could you come and see me tomorrow?
A: I'm afraid I can't tomorrow, but I could on Tuesday.
B: That will suit me perfectly.

A: I'd like to have a long chat with you.
B: Could you spare the time tomorrow?
A: I'm afraid I can't tomorrow, but I could on Thursday.
B: That will suit me admirably.

PRACTICE

A: I'd like to have a long chat with you.
B: Could you . . . 1 tomorrow?
A: I'm afraid I can't tomorrow, but I could . . . 6.
B: That will suit me perfectly/admirably.

1

drop in and see me
call
pay me a visit
visit me
come round to my place
come to tea
manage

6

the day after
on Wednesday
Friday
Saturday
Sunday
Monday
early next week
this afternoon

We could tell her not to

A: I think we'd better not invite Joan to our party.
B: Why not?
A: Because she might bring her dog with her.
B: But we could tell her not to, couldn't we?

A: I think we'd better not invite Mr Jones to our party.
B: Why not?
A: Because he might bring his friend with him.
B: But we could tell him not to, couldn't we?

. . . bring her dog with her.

A: I think we'd better not invite **X** to our party.
B: Why not?
A: Because he/she might . . . **1**.
B: But we could tell him/her not to, couldn't we?

1

stay too late
bring his/her violin
            family   } with him/her
insist on singing
get too noisy
be unsociable as usual
      a wet blanket
want to play silly games

He might be a lecturer

A: How would Harry make his living if he lost his job?
B: He'd probably be a cowboy.
A: Don't you think he might become a university lecturer?
B: No, I don't think that's very likely.

A: How would Vera make her living if she lost her job?
B: She'll probably be a model.
A: Don't you think she might become a barmaid?
B: Yes, perhaps.

PRACTICE

A: How would X make his/her living if he/she lost his/her job?
B: He'd/She'd probably . . . 1.
A: Don't you think he/she might . . . 1?
B: Yes, perhaps. // No, I don't think that's very likely.

1

take up cooking
be a waitress
     jockey
     stable-boy
     doctor
     surgeon
     district nurse
turn artist
     actor/actress
     soldier
     sailor
     farmer
train as a pilot
       surveyor

You might find it too hot

A: I'm going to visit Africa next week.
B: I don't think you'd better.
A: Why not?
B: Because you might find it too hot.

A: I'm going to stay in London by myself next week.
B: I think you'd better not.
A: Why not?
B: Because you might lose your way.

PRACTICE

A: I'm going to . . . 1 next week.
B: I don't think you'd better.//
I think you'd better not.
A: Why not?
B: Because you might . . . 1a.

I'm going to learn mountaineering.

1	1a
give my money away	dislike poverty
spend my savings	bitterly regret it
learn to play poker	lose all your money
mountaineering	not have a good head for heights
leave home	feel miserable
school	need a school-leaving certificate
live in the country	miss town life
sell my car	hate having to walk or take a bus

When she has graduated

A: What's your cousin Helen going to do, when she has graduated?
B: She'll probably get married.
A: And what about Tessa?
B: When she has graduated, she'll probably take a job.
A: What's your brother John going to do, when he has finished school?
B: He'll probably go to the university.
A: And how about Henry?
B: When he has finished school, he'll probably take up journalism.

. . probably take up journalism.

PRACTICE

A: What's **X** going to do, when he/she has . . . **3**?
B: He'll/She'll probably . . . **1**.
A: And what/how about **Y**?
B: When he/she has . . . **3**, he'll/she'll probably . . . **1**.

3	**1**
left the hospital	go into business
moved to the country	take a teacher's diploma
London	join the Army/Navy
got his/her degree	an insurance firm
qualified	study economics
finished training	work in London
resigned his/her present job	on a farm for a time
	get a post in the City
	help his/her father
	be a professional footballer
	golfer
	lawyer
	taxi-driver
	take up nursing
	architecture
	learn accountancy
	shorthand

I shall, as soon as I've had tea

A: Will you be going to town this afternoon?
B: Yes, I shall, as soon as I've finished typing.
A: Will you give me a lift, please?
B: Certainly.

A: Will you be going to town this evening?
B: Yes, I shall, as soon as I've had tea.
A: Will you give me a lift, please?
B: Well, I'm afraid I'm not taking the car.

PRACTICE

A: Will you be going to town this morning/afternoon/evening?
B: Yes, I shall, as soon as I've . . . 3.
A: Will you give me a lift, please?
B: Certainly. // Well, I'm afraid I'm not taking the car.

3

written this letter
prepared my lecture
put the baby to bed
made a pie for supper
read another chapter
seen the TV news
looked at the paper
changed my suit/dress
mended the fence
my stocking
fed the horses
got in the washing

... when I was twenty-one *

A: Uncle made an unusual promise yesterday.
B: What was that?
A: He promised to take me to Paris when he got a rise.
B: That will be nice.

A: Auntie made an unusual promise yesterday.
B: What was that?
A: She promised to give me her gold watch when I was twenty-one.
B: That will be nice.

... take me to India.

PRACTICE

A: Uncle/Auntie made an unusual promise yesterday.
B: What was that?
A: He/She promised to ... **1** when he/she/I ... **2**.
B: That will be nice.

1

buy me a motor bike
        scooter
    us a piano
help me choose a new outfit
pay for my music lessons
    me to spend a week in
                London
come to live near us
take me to India
        America
        Spain
introduce me to the general manager

2

left school
next visited us
got his/her/my promotion
    my degree
    married
retired
passed my exam
came to London

He said he wouldn't – not until he had graduated

A: Will Philip take a job soon, do you think?
B: He said he wouldn't—not until he had graduated.
A: And when will that be?
B: Not for some time.

A: Will Vera leave home soon, do you think?
B: She said she wouldn't—not until she had saved her fare to Australia.
A: And when will that be?
B: Not for some time.

PRACTICE

A: Will **X** . . . **1** soon, do you think?
B: He/She said he/she wouldn't—not until he/she had . . . **3**.
A: And when will that be?
B: Not for some time.

1

buy a car
     bike
visit New York
take up fishing
         golf
         chess
turn professional
go abroad
allow himself/herself a holiday
come down from the university
get married

3

left school
got his/her degree
retired

won a tournament
had his/her book published
redecorated the house
qualified
got promotion

. . . when he had bought a car

A: I hope Harry will keep his promise.
B: What promise?
A: He said he would take me to Venice when he had bought a car. And now he *has* bought a car.
B: Perhaps he's forgotten about it.

A: I hope Ethel will keep her promise.
B: What promise?
A: She said she would teach me French when she had passed her exam. And now she *has* passed the exam.
B: Perhaps she's forgotten about it.

. . . paint my portrait.

PRACTICE

A: I hope **X** will keep his/her promise.
B: What promise?
A: He/She said he/she would **. . . 1** when he/she had **. . . 3**. And now he/she *has* **. . . 3**.
B: Perhaps he's/she's forgotten about it.

1

mend my bicycle
make me a new dress
give me some lessons
pay for my holiday
help me with the garden
paint my portrait
come for a walk
show me his/her stamp collection

3

mended his/her own
made herself one
turned professional
had promotion
finished work
held his/her exhibition
written his/her letters
new book

78

Lately. Last. At last

A: Have you been fishing lately?
B: The last time was in the summer.
A: I went last week and caught a big pike.
B: Oh, so you've got one at last!

A: Have you been shooting lately?
B: The last time was before Christmas.
A: I went last week and shot a big boar.
B: Oh, so you've got one at last!

PRACTICE

A: Have you been . . . **1 + ing** lately?
B: The last time was before Christmas/in the summer.
A: I went last week and . . . **9**.
B: Oh, so you've got one at last!

1 + ing

playing tennis
cycling
motoring
fly fishing

doing any wild life photography
gardening
boxing
swimming

9

bought a new racket
    bicycle
    car
caught a big salmon
    trout
got a close-up of a stag
took an allotment
won a prize
    trophy

She's for ever talking in class

A: The teacher's angry with Jill.
B: Is she really? Why?
A: Because she's for ever talking in class.
B: That must be very annoying.

A: The teacher's angry with Fred.
B: Is he really? Why?
A: Because he's always grinning in class.
B: That must be very annoying.

PRACTICE

A: The teacher's angry with **X**.
B: Is he/she really? Why?
A: Because he's/she's always/for ever . . . **1 + ing**.
B: That must be very annoying.

1 + ing

coming late
being late
falling asleep
copying from other students
making spelling mistakes
giggling
staying away
neglecting his/her homework
playing in class
losing his/her books

Something's always going wrong

A: I'm going to sell my car.
B: Are you really? Why?
A: Because something's always going wrong with it.
B: In that case you'd better get rid of it.

A: I'm going to sell my bicycle.
B: Are you really? Why?
A: Because it keeps on breaking down.
B: In that case you'd better get rid of it.

. . . making a strange noise.

PRACTICE

A: I'm going to sell my . . . **5**.
B: Are you really? Why?
A: Because something's always going wrong with it.
   //it keeps on . . . **1 + ing**.
B: In that case you'd better get rid of it.

5	1 + ing
watch	getting out of order
radio	on my nerves
TV set	sticking
tape recorder	letting me down
record player	stopping
cart	making a strange noise
pen	
fridge	

*I'm washing up every day this month**

A : I'm taking the children to school every day this month.
B : But it's only this month, isn't it?
A : Yes. Next month Dennis'll be taking the children to school and I'll be doing the housework.
B : It's different with us. I always take the children to school and Kate always does the housework.

A : I'm washing up every day this month.
B : But it's only this month, isn't it?
A : Yes. Next month Elsie will be washing up and I'll be cooking the meals.
B : It's different with us. I always cook the meals and Mary always does the washing up.

PRACTICE

A : I'm . . . **1 + ing** every day this month.
B : But it's only this month, isn't it?
A : Yes. Next month **X**'ll be . . . **1 + ing** and I'll be . . . **1 + ing**.
B : It's different with us. I always . . . **1** and **Y** always . . . **1s**.

1 + ing	**1(s)**
making the beds	make(s) the beds
doing the fires	do(es) the fires
cleaning the house/flat/room	clean(s) the house/flat/room
working in the garden	work(s) in the garden
making up the accounts	make(s) up the accounts
minding the shop	mind(s) the shop
doing duty at the bar	do(es) duty at the bar
looking after the refreshments	look(s) after the refreshments
putting the baby to bed	put(s) the baby to bed
getting the supper	get(s) the supper

He's been ringing me up every day

A: I don't know how to get rid of Mr Brown
B: Why do you want to get rid of him?
A: He's been ringing me up every day for the last month.
B: You ought to change your phone number.

A: I don't know how to get rid of Mrs Black.
B: Why do you want to get rid of her?
A: She's been stopping me in the street every day for the last month.
B: You ought to go to town another way.

She's been stopping me in the street . . .

PRACTICE

A: I don't know how to get rid of **X**.
B: Why do you want to get rid of him/her?
A: He's/She's been . . . **1** ı **ing** every day for the last month.
B: You ought to . . . **1**.

1 + ing

coming to see me
       tea
writing me letters
sending me flowers
interrupting my work
borrowing our newspaper
chatting over the garden fence
calling after me in the street

1

ask him/her not to
tell him/her to stop
       leave you alone
send them back
keep your door shut
stop taking one
stay indoors
go to work earlier
    school

She's always talking about herself

A: I've no patience with Susan.
B: Why?
A: Because she's always talking about herself.
B: Then it's high time she was more sensible.

A: I've no patience with John.
B: Why?
A: Because he's always admiring himself.
B: Then it's high time he was more modest.

PRACTICE

A: I've no patience with **X**.
B: Why?
A: Because he's/she's always . . . **1** + **ing**.
B: Then it's high time he/she . . . **2**.

1 + ing

praising himself/herself
making a nuisance of himself/herself
showing pictures of himself/herself
introducing himself/herself as an expert
dressing himself/herself up
looking at himself/herself in the glass
feeling sorry for himself/herself

2

changed his/her ways
was more considerate
    less conceited
grew up a bit
stopped being childish
took a more responsible
    attitude
thought more about other
    people

She wants the garden all to herself

A: Mary is rather selfish.
B: In what way?
A: She wants the garden all to herself.
B: That's very selfish of her indeed.

A: The Jones boys are rather selfish.
B: In what way?
A: They want the ball all to themselves.
B: That's very selfish of them indeed.

They want the ball . . .

PRACTICE

A: **X** is rather selfish.// **X** and **Y** are rather selfish.
A: He/She wants the . . . **5** all to himself/herself.// They want the . . . **5** all to themselves.
B: That's very selfish of him/her/them indeed.

5

house
library
sitting-room
playground
kitchen
newspaper
magazines
workshop
car
puppy
pony

They have only themselves to blame

A: Jack has failed his exam again.
B: I wonder why.
A: Probably because he hasn't been working hard enough.
B: In that case he has only himself to blame.

A: The Smith girls have failed their exams again.
B: I wonder why.
A: Probably because they haven't been really trying.
B: In that case they have only themselves to blame.

PRACTICE

A: **X** has failed his/her exam again.//
   X and **Y** have failed their exams again.
B: I wonder why.
A: Probably because $\left\{ \begin{array}{l} \text{he/she hasn't} \\ \text{they haven't} \end{array} \right\}$ been ... **1 + ing.**

B: In that case $\left\{ \begin{array}{l} \text{he/she has} \\ \text{they have} \end{array} \right\}$ only $\left\{ \begin{array}{l} \text{himself/herself} \\ \text{themselves} \end{array} \right\}$ to blame.

1 + ing

coming to class regularly
doing his/her/their homework properly
                    exercises carefully
       enough reading
learning much
listening to the teacher carefully
going to bed early enough
attending in class
concentrating on his/her/their work

Have you hurt yourself?

A: Why are you gasping?
   Have you hurt yourself?
B: Not very much, thank you.
A: What were you doing?
B: I was trying to raise myself
   on to that branch when I
   fell.

A: Why are you limping?
   Have you hurt yourself?
B: Not very much, thank you.
A: What were you doing?
B: I was trying to cut myself a
   stick when I fell.

. . . through the railings.

PRACTICE

A: Why are you ... **1 + ing**?
   Have you hurt yourself.
B: Not very much, thank you.
A: What were you doing?
B: I was trying to ... **1** when
   I fell.

1 + ing	**1**
groaning	squeeze myself through the railings
crying	make myself run faster
pulling faces	lower myself down that hole
swearing	lift myself over the bar
looking pale	get myself a flower for my button-hole
red	stop myself slipping
	save myself from being run over

I can't force myself to do so

A: I'm terribly hard up.
B: Why don't you economize?
A: I know I ought to, but I can't force myself to do so.
B: Then you have only yourself to blame.

A: We're terribly hard up.
B: Why don't you live more simply?
A: We know we ought to, but we can't bring ourselves to do so.
B: Then you have only yourselves to blame.

We're terribly hard up.

PRACTICE

A: I'm terribly hard up.
   We're
B: Why don't you . . . 1?
A: I/We know I/we ought to, but I/we can't force/bring myself/ourselves to do so.
B: Then you have only yourself/yourselves to blame.

1

take a job/jobs
      some work home
start work
move to cheaper digs
work overtime
give up smoking
have fewer luxuries
sell your car
budget more carefully
spend less on luxuries

88

We didn't enjoy ourselves much

A: We went to a dance last night, but we didn't enjoy ourselves much.
B: Why not?
A: Because we didn't like the band.
B: Well, you can't always enjoy yourselves.

A: I went to a party last night, but I didn't enjoy myself much.
B: Why not?
A: Because I didn't like the people.
B: Perhaps you'll enjoy yourself more next time.

PRACTICE

A: I/We went to a dance/party last night, but I/we didn't enjoy myself/ourselves much.
B: Why not?
A: Because I/we . . . **2**.
B: Well, you can't always enjoy yourself/yourselves. // Perhaps you'll enjoy yourself/yourselves more next time.

2

drunk too much
danced too long
played too many rough games
got very tired
        sleepy
        bored
quarrelled with **X**
disliked the other guests
stayed too late
had bad hands at cards

She was so cross that I didn't speak*

A : Did you talk to Charles
yesterday?
B : No, not very much.
A : Why not?
B : Because he was in such a
bad mood that I let him
alone.

A : Did you talk to Edna yes-
terday?
B : No, not very much.
A : Why not?
B : Because she was so cross
that I didn't dare to.

Because she was so cross . . .

PRACTICE

A : Did you talk to X yesterday?
B : No, not very much.
A : Why not?
B : Because he/she was $\begin{cases} \text{so } \ldots \textbf{ 4} & \text{that I didn't dare to.} \\ \text{in such a(an) } \ldots \textbf{ 5} & \text{let him/her alone.} \end{cases}$

4	5
angry	ugly temper
sulky	bad frame of mind
busy	temper
spiteful	mad hurry
moody	furious rush
sullen	state of nerves
bad tempered	

He did it himself

A: Henry is very clever. He has constructed a steam engine.
B: Who helped him?
A: Nobody. He did it himself.
B: That's very clever of him indeed.

A: The White sisters are very clever. They have won a competition.
B: Who helped them?
A: Nobody. They did it themselves.
B: That's very clever of them indeed.

PRACTICE

A: **X** is// **X** and **Y** are very clever.
   He/She has// They have . . . **3**.
B: Who helped him/her/them?
A: Nobody.   He/She/They did it himself/herself/themselves.
B: That's very clever of him/her/them indeed.

3

built a bungalow
written a play
composed a symphony
invented a duplicating machine
            new method of teaching
designed a shopping centre
constructed a motor-cycle
                radio-set
                rocket
developed a new sort of rose
bred a new kind of pig

They told me themselves

A: Arthur is going to take a trip round the world.
B: Who told you?
A: *He* did himself.
B: I don't quite believe it myself.

A: The Smiths are going to stand for Parliament.
B: Who told you?
A: *They* did themselves.
B: I don't quite believe it myself.

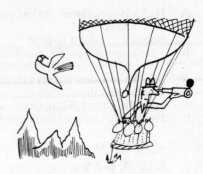

. . . *a trip round the world.*

PRACTICE

A: **X** is//**X** and **Y** are going to . . . **1**.
B: Who told you?
A: *He/She./They* did himself/herself/themselves,
B. I don't quite believe it myself.

1

take a trip to South America
buy a big yacht
study theology
make a fortune in five years
write a best-selling novel
turn professional footballer(s)
emigrate
resign his/her/their job(s)

We did everything ourselves

A : Who painted the room?
B : Henry and I.
A : Did anyone help you?
B : No. We did everything ourselves.

A : Who stopped the chimney smoking?
B : Tom and I.
A : Did anyone help you?
B : No. We did it ourselves.

PRACTICE

A : Who . . . 2?
B : X and I.
A : Did anyone help you?
B : No. We did it/everything ourselves.

2

did up the house so nicely
redecorated the house
refurnished the house
designed the garden so beautifully
planted the garden
laid the new lawn so well
put up the new curtains
    in the central heating
tiled the bathroom
prepared dinner so well

You must make it yourself

A: I could do with a cup of tea.
B: If you want tea, you must make it yourself. I haven't time.
A: I don't mind making it myself.
B: All right. You'll find everything in the kitchen.

A: I could do with a cheese sandwich.
B: If you want a cheese sandwich, you must get it yourself. I haven't time.
A: I don't mind getting it myself.
B: All right. You'll find everything in the kitchen.

. . . everything in the kitchen.

PRACTICE

A: I could do with a(an) . . . **5**.
B: If you want a(an) . . . **5**, you must make/get it yourself. I haven't time.
A: I don't mind making/getting it myself.
B: All right. You'll find everything in the kitchen.

5
cup of coffee
  hot milk
sandwich
fried steak and onions
glass of lemonade
  tomato juice
omelette
good supper
fresh salad
plate of bacon and eggs
bowl of soup
long cold drink

The others haven't arrived, though they've got a car

A: So you found your way all right!
B: Yes, I managed it, although I haven't got a car.
A: Some of the others haven't arrived, though they've got a car.
B: I think I hear them coming now.

A: So you found your way all right!
B: Yes, I managed it, although it's quite dark.
A: Some of the others haven't arrived, though they've been here before.
B: I think I hear them coming now.

. . . it's very foggy.

PRACTICE

A: So you found your way all right!
B: Yes, I managed it, although . . . **9**.
A: Some of the others haven't arrived, though they . . . **9a**.
B: I think I hear them coming now.

9

it's snowing
   very foggy
the road's not well sign-posted
I haven't got a map
it's so long since my last visit
I've had to walk
the road is up
I've never been here before
   a long way to come

9a

set out early, I think
live quite near
should know the way
've got a map
   been here several times before
   got bicycles
said they would start early
know the way well
don't have far to come

95

. . . though he's not bad at heart

A: I've no patience with Bill.
B: What's the matter?
A: He will smoke continuously, though I've often told him not to.
B: I know. He behaves foolishly, though he's not bad at heart.

A: I've no patience with Jane.
B: What's the matter?
A: She will wear that queer hat, though I've often asked her not to.
B: I know. She behaves strangely, though she's not bad at heart.

PRACTICE

A: I've no patience with **X**.
B: What's the matter?
A: He/She will **. . . 1**, though I've often told/asked him/her not to.
B: I know. He/She behaves foolishly/strangely, though he's/she's not bad at heart.

1

stay up late
remain in the water too long
neglect his/her homework
play truant
lie in bed half the day
go out without a coat
dress untidily
play cards half the night
spend all his/her money on pop records

Although the room was terribly cold . . .

A: I went to see John yesterday. I *was* surprised by
what I found.
B: What did you find?
A: Although the room was
terribly cold, he was sitting
without his coat on.
B: Oh, that's just like him.

A: I went to see Joan yesterday. I *was* surprised by
what I found.
B: What did you find?
A: Although the room was extremely untidy, she was
doing nothing about it.
B: Oh, that's just like her.

. . . the room was terribly cold.

PRACTICE

A: I went to see **X** yesterday. I *was* surprised by what I found.
B: What did you find?
A: Although the room was . . . **4**, he/she was . . . **1 + ing**.
B: Oh, that's just like him/her.

4	**1 + ing**
quite dark	quietly doing crossword puzzles
full of smoke	playing chess by himself/herself
very chilly	sitting with hardly anything on
dirty	the window open
draughty	closed
quite unfurnished	without a fire
extremely hot	with his/her coat on
	lying asleep on the floor
	playing the piano
	reading a book

I like films which end happily

A: I like films which end happily.
B: And I like films which keep me in suspense.
A: So does Bill.
B: And Jill likes films which are very sentimental.

A: I like gardens that have lots of trees and shrubs.
B: And I like gardens that are full of flowers.
A: So does Mary.
B: And Mother likes gardens that have mostly roses.

PRACTICE

A: I like . . . **5** which/that . . . **9**.
B: And I like . . . **5** which/that . . . **9**.
A: So does **X**.
B: And **Y** likes . . . **5** which/that . . . **9**.

5	**9**
books plays shows novels stories	end unhappily move quickly deal with economic problems philosophical historical describe other countries make one laugh cry think have lots of characters plenty of action
dogs pets	are well trained can be cuddled guard the house live out of doors have short coats don't bark much don't bite postmen

A man who became a teacher

A: I've just read a very good book.

B: What was it about?

A: About a man who became a teacher, but gave it up.

B: And I've just read one about a man that wanted to get rich at all costs.

A: I've just read a good story.

B: What was it about?

A: About a woman who was made President.

B: And I've just read one about a woman who saved Rome.

. . . flew the first aeroplane.

PRACTICE

A: I've just . . . **3**.

B: What was it about?

A: About a man/woman who . . . **2**.

B: And I've just read/seen one about a man/woman who/that

3	**2**
read a good novel	became a doctor
seen a good film	film star
play	missionary
	famous dancer
	skater
	crossed the Atlantic on a raft
	explored the African forest
	went right up the Amazon
	sailed alone round the world
	flew the first aeroplane
	made a rocket flight
	walked across Asia
	invented a thought machine
	refused to pay income tax
	gave away millions

Do I know the person you were talking to?

A: Do I know the person (who) you were talking to just now?
B: I think so. He is the man who brought our dog home.
A: Does he live near here?
B: Yes. He lives in the house which is up for sale.

A: Do I know the person (who) you were talking to just now?
B: I think so. She is the woman who sat next to us in the cinema.
A: Does she live near here?
B: Yes. She lives in the house which belonged to grandfather.

. . . a win on the football pools.

PRACTICE

A: Do I know the person (who) you were talking to just now?
B: I think so. He/She is the man / woman who . . . **2**.
A: Does he/she live near here?
B: Yes. He/She lives in the house which . . . **9**.

2

sold us the roses
laid down our lawn
found the lost bicycle
owned the taxi
    beautiful garden
grew the lovely roses
had a win on the football pools
used to be our neighbour

9

stands on the hill
    in its own ground
has a lovely garden
    long drive
    verandah at the side
overlooks the park
    sea
used to belong to **X**
was built by **X**
is built of stone

It was Jane who helped us

A: I think Jane is rather unfriendly.
B: You mustn't say that.
A: But she is.
B: Don't forget that it was Jane who helped us when we were in difficulties.

A: I think Bill is rather selfish.
B: You mustn't say that.
A: But he is.
B: Don't forget that it was Bill who lent you his bicycle when you were without one.

PRACTICE

A: I think **X** is rather unfriendly/selfish.
B: You mustn't say that.
A: But he/she is.
B: Don't forget that it was **X** who . . . **2** when we/you were . . . **4**.

2

came to see you/us
gave you/us clothes
           food
           somewhere to live
           hospitality
helped with the garden
painted the house
built the greenhouse
advised you/us
did the housework
ran all the errands

4

ill
stranded
in hospital
out of a job
convalescent
down with flu
short of capital
living in the country
laid up

The one you wore last Sunday

A: Which hat ought I to put on?

B: The one (that) you wore last Sunday?

A: Hadn't I better put on the one I bought yesterday?

B: Well, you must make up your own mind.

A: Which coat ought I to put on?

B: The one (which) you had altered?

A: Hadn't I better put on the one I bought last year?

B: Well, you must make up your own mind

Which hat?

PRACTICE

A: Which . . . **5** ought I to put on?

B: The one (that/which) you . . . **2**?

A: Hadn't I better put on the one I . . . **2**?

B: Well, you must make up your own mind.

5	2
dress	bought last Monday
suit	week
blouse	the other day
shirt	in the sale
pullover	got from **X**
raincoat	had for my/your birthday
tie	made for Easter
skirt	for the holidays
costume	the summer
	given to me/you yesterday
	always wear

She is the woman we met at Henry's*

A: There is an article by Mrs Wood in to-day's paper.
B: I don't think I know anyone of that name.
A: She is the woman we met at Henry's last Tuesday.
B: Oh yes, now I remember. The one who was talking about politics.

A: There is an article by Professor Jones in today's paper.
B: I don't think I know anyone of that name.
A: He is the man we heard lecturing last week.
B: Oh yes, now I remember. The one who was criticising the Government.

PRACTICE

A: There is an article by **X** in today's paper.
B: I don't think I know anyone of that name.
A: He/She is the man/woman we ... **2** ... **6**.
B: Oh yes, now I remember. The one who was ... **1 + ing**.

2

met at the Browns'
    Mary's
    the party
  on holiday
got to know in the hotel
shared a taxi with

6

this morning
yesterday
last Sunday
    Monday
    summer
at the weekend
    Easter
a few days ago

1 + ing
riding a tricycle
mending the fence
wearing a smart suit
    old clothes
    horn rimmed spectacles
talking about farming
    bird watching
    sweet peas
in a loud voice
making jokes all the time

About a piece of advice I was given

A : What are you thinking about?
B : About a piece of advice I was given yesterday.
A : Tell me about it.
B : Oh, I don't think it would be very interesting

A : What are you thinking about?
B : About the instructions I received at the office today.
A : Tell me about it.
B : Oh, I don't think it would be very interesting.

a piece of advice I was given.

PRACTICE

A : What are you thinking about?
B : About . . . **5**.
A : Tell me about it.
B : Oh, I don't think it would be very interesting.

5

a bit of information I received yesterday
book I was reading recently
piece of furniture I bought/sold yesterday
poetry/prose I learned by heart
an item of news I read/saw in the papers today
my part in the new play we are going to produce
something my husband/wife/mother told me just now
the way my neighbour uses his garden

Have you seen the book I brought?

A : Have you seen the book I brought from town?
B : No, I haven't.
A : I think I must show it to Kate.
B : Yes, you'd better. She's always interested in things you bring from town.

A : Have you seen the stool I made at woodwork class?
B : No, I haven't.
A : I think I must show it to John.
B : Yes, you'd better. He's always interested in things you make at woodwork class.

PRACTICE

A : Have you seen the . . . 5 I . . . 2?
B : No, I haven't.
A : I think I must show it to **X**.
B : Yes, you'd better. He's/She's always interested in things you . . . 9.

5	2	9
pen	bought	buy
album	got from Jane	get from Jane
camera	Jack	Jack
watch	America	America
parcel	made at pottery class	make at pottery class
bowl	grew in my garden	grow in your garden
rose	won at school	win at school
prize	athletics	athletics
cup	had at Christmas	have at Christmas
presents		

I said I was very tired

A: I'm very tired.
B: What did you say?
A: I said I was very tired.
B: I never knew you when you weren't!

A: I'm very worried.
B: What did you say?
A: I said I was very worried.
B: I never knew you when you weren't!

PRACTICE

I'm very worried.

A: I'm very . . . **4**.
B: What did you say?
A: I said I was very . . . **4**.
B: I never knew you when you weren't!

4

sleepy
busy
happy
sad
hungry
thirsty
depressed
short of money
pleased with myself
unhappy in my work

He said he had just got married

A: When did you last see Mr Green?
B: Last summer. He said he had just got married.
A: Did he really say that?
B: Yes, he did. He said, " I've just got married."

A: When did you last see Mrs Watson?
B: Last year. She said she was going to move house again.
A: Did she really say that?
B: Yes, she did. She said, " I'm going to move house again."

PRACTICE

A: When did you last see **X**?
B: Last ... **6** He/She said he/she had just ... **3**.//
                      was going to ... **1**.
A: Did he/she really say that?
B: Yes, he/she did. He/She said, " I've just ... **3**."//
                          " I'm going to ... **1**."

6	**3**	**1**
spring	got his/her/my degree	take up painting
autumn	bought a car	settle down in England
winter	won a prize	emigrate
week	competition	buy a farm
Christmas	come back from Australia	set up a nursery
Easter	America	grow flowers for a living
summer holidays	written a book	retire
weekend	play	
Sunday	changed his/her/my job	
	retired	

Jim asked me if he should wash the car

A : Jim asked me if he should wash the car.
B : What exactly did he say?
A : He said, " Shall I wash the car? "
B : I think he ought to.

A : Sarah asked me if she should look for another job.
B : What exactly did she say?
A : She said, " Shall I look for another job? "
B : I don't think she ought to.

PRACTICE

A : **X** asked me if he/she should **. . . 1**.
B : What exactly did he/she say?
A : He/She said, " Shall I **. . . 1**? "
B : I (don't) think he/she ought to.

1

start cutting the corn
     picking the apples
buy a car/motor bike
join the Army/Navy/Air Force
go to church
     the university
spend longer on his/her/my homework
leave school
take the dog for a run
put the children to bed
water the garden

It's reasonable that he should *

A : What do you think of Mr White's plan to go to India?
B : I think it's reasonable that he should.
A : I'm glad you approve of his plan.
B : I can't see any reason why I shouldn't.

A : What do you think of Mrs Smith's plan to keep chickens?
B : I think it's very good that she should.
A : I'm glad you approve of her plan.
B : I can't see any reason why I shouldn't.

. . . to alter the garden.

PRACTICE

A : What do you think of **X**'s plan to . . . **1**?
B : I think it's . . . **4** that he/she should.
A : I'm glad you approve of his/her plan.
B : I can't see any reason why I shouldn't.

1
take another job
  a degree
write a novel
do voluntary youth work
learn Russian
  to dance
    ride
study economics
   history
join the golf club
   tennis
alter the garden
   sitting room

4
understandable
sensible
advisable
natural

So that his wife can have a fur coat

A : Mr Green is saving very hard.
B : What for?
A : So that his wife can have a fur coat.
B : I wish there were more unselfish people like that!

A : Mrs Wilson is working very hard.
B : What for?
A : So that her poor relations can have a seaside holiday.
B : I wish there were more unselfish people like that!

PRACTICE

A : **X** is saving/working very hard.
B : What for?
A : So that his/her . . . **5** can . . . **1**.
B : I wish there were more unselfish people like that!

5

sister Kate
brother Bill
friend Jack/Jill
cousin Jane/John
husband
clubmates
family
widowed sister's children

1

buy a bicycle
  TV set
join him/her on a trip to India
afford to go to Cambridge
go to university
finish his/her/their training
have some toys for Christmas
  a car
  fishing rod
  tennis racket

So that her mother will be pleased

A: Eva has managed to become the best scientist in the school.
B: Has she really? That was clever of her.
A: Yes, she has done it so that her mother will be pleased.
B: I see.

A: Fred has managed to become the best footballer in the school.
B: Has he really? That was clever of her.
A: Yes, he has done it so that his teacher will think more of him.
B: I see.

. . . the best scientist in the school.

PRACTICE

A: **X** has managed to become the best **. . . 5** in the school.
B: Has he/she really? That was clever of him/her.
A: Yes, he/she has done it so that his/her **. . . 5a** will **. . . 1**.
B: I see.

5	5a	1
pupil	father	be proud of him/her
student	friends	give him/her a nice present
athlete	headmaster	take him/her on a trip to Italy
tennis player	parents	let him/her go to (the) university
rugby player	brother	drama school
singer	sister	become a professional
actor/actress		
linguist		

So that her mother would be pleased*

A: Last year Fred managed to become the best footballer in the school.
B: Did he really? He did very well then.
A: Yes, he did it so that he could captain the first team.
B: Oh, I see.

A: Last year Mary managed to become the best needlewoman in the school.
B: Did she really? She did very well then.
A: Yes, she did it so that her mother would be pleased.
B: Oh, I see.

PRACTICE

A: Last year **X** managed to become the best **. . . 5** in the school.
B: Did he/she really? He/She did very well then.
A: Yes, he/she did it so that **. . . 9**.
B: Oh, I see.

5	**9**
linguist	his/her parents would give him/her more pocket money
athlete	teacher would be proud of him/her
runner	he/she could become a professional
boxer	could beat his/her brother's record
painter	could have his/her photo in the paper
mathematician	would get his/her name on the honours board
singer	would be mentioned in the school magazine
tennis player	

So as to see the world

A: Victor wants to be a sailor.
B: Why a sailor?
A: So as to see the world, I expect.
B: I wonder if he'll manage it.

A: Diana wants to be an actress.
B: Why an actress?
A: So as to get the limelight, I expect.
B: I wonder if she'll manage it.

So as to be famous . . .

PRACTICE

A: **X** wants to be a(an) **. . . 5**.
B: Why a(an) **. . . 5**?
A: So as to **. . . 1**, I expect.
B: I wonder if he'll/she'll manage it.

5	1
astronaut	go round the world
pilot	be famous
atomic scientist	get rich
doctor	help other people
member of parliament	explore outer space
stockbroker	make a fortune
opera singer	become important
surgeon	
band leader	
conductor	

So as not to have to walk

A : Fred has bought a bicycle.
B : What ever for?
A : So as not to have to walk to work.
B : It seems a reasonable thing to do.

A : Phyllis has bought a sewing machine.
B : What ever for?
A : So as not to have to pay for dressmaking.
B : It seems a reasonable thing to do.

PRACTICE

A : **X** has bought a(an) **. . . 5**.
B : What ever for?
A : So as not to **. . . 1**.
B : It seems a reasonable thing to do.

5	**1**
house	live in a flat any more
car	spend so much on taxis
motor boat	be always in a crowd
sailing boat	borrowing Jack's/Elsie's
umbrella	get wet so often
do-it-yourself kit	have nothing to do at home
	anything out of order at home
electric razor	cut himself so often
home hair dryer	pay for having her hair set

114

He asked me not to come late

A: What did Mr Jones want?
B: He asked me not to come late to work.
A: I told you last week to be more punctual, you know.
B: Yes, I really must try to.

A: What did Mrs Smith want?
B: She wanted me not to make so many mistakes.
A: I told you last week to be more careful, you know.
B: Yes, I really must try to.

... behave better.

PRACTICE

A: What did **X** want?
B: He/She asked/wanted me not to ... **1**.
A: I told you last week to ... **1a**, you know.
B: Yes, I really must try to.

1	1a
forget the washing-up	keep the house tidy
my lesson again	be less forgetful
leave my desk so untidy	more tidy
bike on the path	put it in the shed
talk so much in class	be quieter
shout in the playground	behave better
do such bad homework	work harder
push to the front of the line	keep in the queue

Bill ought to have paid

A: Jack's annoyed with Bill.
B: Is he really? Why?
A: He says Bill ought to have paid him back his money yesterday.
B: I agree with Jack about that.

A: Jill's cross with Jane.
B: Is she really? Why?
A: She says Jane should have asked permission to take her stockings yesterday.
B: I agree with Jill about that.

PRACTICE

A: **X**'s offended/cross with **Y**.
B: Is he/she really? Why?
A: He/She says **Y** ought to/should have **. . . 3** yesterday.
B: I agree with **X** about that.

3

returned his/her book
left him/her a message
taken more care of his/her records
                              bicycle
asked leave to borrow his/her book
                              tennis racket
                              gramophone
warned him/her about the change of plan
waited for him/her after school
saved him/her some of the sandwiches
helped in the garden
          with the washing up
                    ironing
passed the ball more often

She might have forgotten

A : Why didn't Joan come to see us yesterday?
B : I've no idea. She might have forgotten all about it.
A : Or she might have gone to see her aunt.
B : She probably did.

A : Why didn't Bill come to see us yesterday?
B : I've no idea. He might have had trouble with his car.
A : Or he might have worked in the garden.
B : He probably did.

PRACTICE

A : Why didn't **X** come to see us yesterday?
B : I've no idea. He/She might have **. . . 3**.
A : Or he/she might have **. . . 3**.
B : He/She probably did.

3

overslept
had a crash again
been mending his car/bike/scooter
gone to the football match
     sports meeting
     flower show
     dog show
     agricultural show
thought the weather unsuitable
played golf
   tennis
gone swimming
   sailing
felt too ill
   tired
   lazy
   busy

He must have gone to the pictures*

A : So Fred hasn't come to class today.
B : I'm not surprised. It's happened before.
A : Do you think he's ill?
B : No, I think he must have gone to the pictures.

A : So Vera hasn't visited us today.
B : I'm not surprised. It's happened before.
A : Do you think she's ill?
B : No, I think she must have gone bathing.

. . . to the pictures.

PRACTICE

A : So **X** hasn't//**X** and **Y** haven't . . . **3** today.
B : I'm not surprised. It's happened before.
A : Do you think he's/she's/they're ill?
B : No, I think he/she/they must have . . . **3a**.

3

been to see us
done his/her/their homework
    the housework
taken the dog for a run
tidied up the house
helped with the cooking
come to lessons
    music lessons

3a

gone harvesting
   on holiday
   skating
   blackberrying
   mushrooming
stayed at home to work
forgotten about it
broken his/her/their bicycle(s) again
had a puncture
    visitors
started planting up the garden
been put off by the thunder
              rain
             bad weather

118

He's said to have won a lottery

A: Henry has been spending a lot of money lately.
B: Yes, he's said to have won a lottery.
A: Really? He keeps very quiet about it.
B: Quite. He must be afraid of being robbed.

A: Mary has been spending a lot of money lately.
B: Yes, she's said to have come into a fortune.
A: Really? She keeps very quiet about it.
B: Quite. She must be afraid of getting begging letters.

PRACTICE

A: **X** has been spending a lot of money lately.
B: Yes, he's/she's said to have **. . . 3**.
A: Really? He/She keeps very quiet about it.
B: Quite. He/She must be afraid of **. . . 1 + ing**.

3

inherited a legacy
done well on the Stock Exchange
had a win on the football pools
been very successful in business
backed some good horses

1 + ing

being asked for a loan
kidnapped
known to be rich
having too many friends
borrowers
losing it
drawing attention to it

You needn't have done that

A: Why did you play cards so late yesterday?
B: Because I wanted to relax.
A: Oh, but you needn't have done that. You could have gone for a walk.
B: I'm tired of going for walks.

A: Why did you watch TV so long yesterday?
B: Because I wanted to relax.
A: Oh, but you didn't need to do that. You could have gone to the club.
B: I'm tired of going to the club so often.

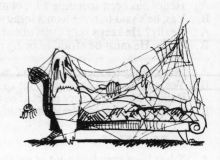

. . . on the sofa so long.

PRACTICE

A: Why did you . . . **1** yesterday?
B: Because I wanted to relax.
A: Oh, but you needn't have done//didn't need to do that. You could have gone for a walk// to the club.
B: I'm tired of going for walks//to the club so often.

1

read so long
dance so much
go to see **X**
  the pub
play bridge so late
  the piano so long
   gramophone so long
lie on the beach so long
   sofa so long
sit knitting so long

120

I'd have visited Edinburgh

A : How did you spend your last summer holidays?
B : I went to Brighton.
A : Would you have stayed in London if you hadn't gone to Brighton?
B : No, I wouldn't. I'd have visited Edinburgh.

A : How did you spend your last Christmas holidays?
B : I stayed at home.
A : Would you have gone to your cousin's if you hadn't stayed at home?
B : No, I wouldn't. I'd have gone to my grandmother's.

PRACTICE

A : How did you spend your last summer / Christmas holidays?
B : I . . . 2.
A : Would you have . . . 3 if you hadn't . . . 3?
B : No, I wouldn't. I'd have . . . 3.

2

visited stayed in took a trip to	Paris New York Florida the mountains the lakes Ireland Cornwall Scotland Wales Madeira
3 gone to visited stayed in taken a trip to	

What would you have done if . . .

A : We planted early potatoes
in that piece of ground.
B : What would you have
done if you hadn't got the
seed?
A : We'd probably have put in
late crop potatoes.
B : Would those have done
well, do you think?
A : Oh, yes.

A : We planted winter wheat
in that field.
B : What would you have
done if you hadn't got the
seed?
A : We'd probably have put in
spring barley.
B : Would that have done
well, do you think?
A : Oh, yes.

Would carrots have done well . . .

PRACTICE

A : We planted **. . . 5** in that field/piece of ground.
B : What would you have done if you hadn't got the seed?
A : We'd probably have put in **. . . 5**.
B : Would that/those have done well, do you think?
A : Oh, yes.

5
maize
beetroot
spinach
artichokes
flax
rye
onions
clover
parsnips
peas
beans
carrots

You might have been hurt

A: I'm glad you didn't take that trip yesterday.
B: Why?
A: Because you might have been hurt in the railway crash.
B: Oh, I don't think it would have been as bad as all that.

A: I'm glad you didn't go sailing yesterday.
B: Why?
A: Because you might have been upset in a squall.
B: Oh, I don't think it would have been as bad as all that.

PRACTICE

A: I'm glad you didn't . . . **1** yesterday.
B: Why?
A: Because you might have . . . **3**.
B: Oh, I don't think it would have been as bad as all that.

1

go to the theatre
    and see **X**
    shooting
    fishing
    climbing
    riding
    swimming
    hiking
    camping
play cards

3

got drowned
    wounded
    lost in the forest
    caught in the storm
    wet through
been very sorry
            disappointed
had a bad fall
caught a cold
            fever
lost a lot of money

You could have seen a film

A: It's a pity you insisted on staying at home last night.
B: Why?
A: Because you could have seen a very good film at the Odeon.
B: But if I hadn't stayed at home I might have got caught in the storm.

A: It's a pity you insisted on staying at home yesterday.
B: Why?
A: Because you could have had a lovely walk in the country.
B: But if I hadn't stayed at home I might have had too much work today.

. . . met a lot of interesting people at the Joneses.

PRACTICE

A: It's a pity you insisted on staying at home last night/yesterday.
B: Why?
A: Because you could have . . . **3**.
B: But if I hadn't stayed at home I might have . . . **3a**.

3	**3a**
seen a good play at the theatre	got wet through
enjoyed yourself at the party	arrived home very late
met a lot of interesting people at the Joneses	spent too much money
had a good game of bridge	missed meeting **X**
watched an excellent sports meeting	disappointed the children
the show jumping	been very tired

I wish he would take me to Paris

A: I'd like Father to take me on a trip to Paris.
B: I wish he would take me to Scotland, fishing.
A: Do you think he will?
B: It's not very likely, but I do wish he would.

A: I'd like Mother to buy me a smart costume.
B: I wish she would buy me a party frock.
A: Do you think she will?
B: It's not very likely, but I do wish she would.

. . . give me a pony.

PRACTICE

A: I'd like Father/Mother to . . . **1**.
B: I wish he/she would . . . **1**.
A: Do you think he/she will?
B: It's not very likely, but I do wish he/she would.

1

buy me a new bicycle
    scooter
    small car
    boat
    sailing dinghy
    house
send me away to school
    to a music school
    drama school

let me go nursing
    farming
    to sea
    America
give me an allowance
    a pony
join the tennis club
    social club

I wish I had a car

A : I wish I had a car.
B : Why do you want one just now?
A : To take part in the rally tomorrow.
B : I wish I could help you, but I can't.

A : I wish I had a ski outfit.
B : Why do you want one just now?
A : To go for a holiday in Switzerland.
B : I wish I could help you, but I can't.

PRACTICE

A : I wish I had a . . . **5**.
B : Why do you want one just now?
A : To . . . **1**.
B : I wish I could help you, but I can't.

5	**1**
yacht	go on a summer cruise
sailing boat	learn to sail in
set of golf clubs	play golf with
piano	practise on
good violin	get a richer tone in playing
large garden	grow lots of flowers
farm	breed horses
typewriter	copy out my notes

I wish the plumber hadn't come

A: I wish the plumber hadn't come today.
B: What would you have done if he hadn't?
A: I'd have gone to the beach.
B: Yes, no doubt that would have been more interesting.

A: I wish the district nurse hadn't come today.
B: What would you have done if she hadn't?
A: I'd have done all the housework.
B: Yes, no doubt that would have been more satisfactory.

I wish the plumber hadn't come today.

PRACTICE

A: I wish . . . 5 hadn't come today.
B: What would you have done if he/she/they hadn't?
A: I'd have . . . 3.
B: Yes, no doubt that would have been more interesting/satisfactory.

5

the builder
decorator
gardener
sanitary inspector
people next door
vicar
my cousin
Uncle **X**
Aunt **Y**
our neighbours

3

made some jam
         cakes
watched TV
worked in the garden
done my essay
        homework
the laundry
      ironing
finished my novel
washed my hair
gone for a swim

I shan't have done it till Monday

A: Would you care to come round and see me this week?
B: I'm afraid I'm very busy this week. I'm writing an important essay.
A: Won't you have finished it by Saturday?
B: No, I shan't have finished it till Monday.

A: Would you care to come round and see me this week?
B: I'm afraid I'm very busy this week. I'm doing a difficult experiment.
A: Won't you have done it by tomorrow?
B: No, I shan't have done it till Monday.

PRACTICE

A: Would you care to come round and see me this week?
B: I'm afraid I'm very busy this week. I'm ... 1 + ing.
A: Won't you have done/finished it by Saturday/tomorrow?
B: No, I shan't have done/finished it till Monday.

1 + ing

writing a review for a magazine
   an important article
doing some laboratory work
finishing my diploma paper
    work
preparing a report for my boss
getting ready for the meeting
stocktaking at the club
studying for my exams
spring-cleaning
redecorating the sitting-room
mending our roof

128

I'll probably have left . . .

A: Will you be coming here on Tuesday?
B: By Tuesday I'll probably have left for Australia.
A: What shall I do with myself when you've gone?
B: You'll probably find plenty to do.

A: Will you be coming here on Mother's birthday?
B: By Mother's birthday I'll probably have gone abroad.
A: What shall I do with myself when you've gone?
B: You'll probably find plenty to do.

. . . gone to live in Wales.

PRACTICE

A: Will you be coming here . . . 6?
B: By . . . 6 I'll probably have . . . 3.
A: What shall I do with myself when you've gone?
B: You'll probably find plenty to do.

6

(on) Monday
the day after tomorrow
next Wednesday
next week
(on) the 10th
    Christmas Day
    Easter bank holiday

3

left the district
gone to live in Scotland
              Wales
              Ireland
              the North of England
taken up my job in London
                  Bristol
begun my holidays
moved to the country
finished my stay here

I can't bear to think . . .

A: What's all that stuff in the hall?
B: That's the new wall paper for the sitting-room.
A: I can't bear to think of your doing it all by yourself.
B: Perhaps Uncle George will help.

A: What's all that stuff in the garden?
B: That's the manure for spreading.
A: I can't bear to think of your doing it all by yourself.
B: Perhaps young Bill will help.

PRACTICE

A: What's all that stuff . . . **7**.
B: That's . . . **5**.
A: I can't bear to think of your doing it all by yourself.
B: Perhaps **X** will help.

7	**5**
on the stairs	the week's washing to be done
lawn	dressing for digging into the garden
in the yard	paint for the decorating
road	**X**'s dirty football gear for washing
bedroom	a load of coal to bring in
kitchen	rubbish to be burnt
by the gate	creosote to paint the fence with
fence	mending to be done

In London (I)

LONDONER: This is St. James's Park.

VISITOR: What building is that?

LONDONER: That's Buckingham Palace, with the Queen Victoria Memorial in front. Behind us is Wellington Barracks. That road leads to Trafalgar Square.

VISITOR: Can one go anywhere in the park?

LONDONER: Yes, anywhere where there are no railings.

... anywhere where there are no railings.

Would you like to sit on the grass, or on this seat?

VISITOR: Yes, let's sit down. I like watching the scene. What are those children doing, running about in bathing costumes?

LONDONER: They're playing in the sandpit, and on the amusement machines.

PRACTICE

LONDONER: This is ... 5.

VISITOR: What building is that?

LONDONER: That's ... 5a with ... 5b in front//to the right/left.

VISITOR: What are those people doing?

LONDONER: They're ... 9.

5	5a	5b
Hyde Park	Marble Arch	Speakers' Corner
Kensington Gardens	the Albert Hall	the Albert Memorial
Trafalgar Square	National Gallery	Admiralty Arch
Parliament Square	Houses of Parliament	Westminster Abbey
the Embankment	Festival Hall	County Hall

9

music lovers, booking seats for a concert
office workers, having lunch in the open air
                enjoying the sunshine in their lunch hour
visitors, feeding the pigeons
            watching the changing of the guard
foreigners, taking photographs

131

In London (II)

FATHER: What did you show Ian and Sheila in London today?

JANE: First we went to the Tower, and saw the collection of armour and the Crown Jewels. Ian said he liked the Beefeaters best, but Sheila thought the Crown Jewels were most interesting.

JOHN: While we were by the river we saw Tower Bridge opening for a big ship to come through.

JANE: Then we walked to the Monument and went up. We had a good view from the top.

JOHN: And we saw the porters in Billingsgate Market carrying fish baskets on their heads.

FATHER: Did you take your friends to St. Paul's Cathedral?

JANE: Oh yes. Sheila and I went up as far as the Whispering Gallery.

JOHN: Ian and I went right up as far as we could, to the top of the dome and cross.

PRACTICE

FATHER: What did you show X in London today?

JANE: We . . . 9.

JOHN: And we . . . 9.

JANE: Then we . . . 9.

JOHN: Then we went by tube to . . . 5 and. . . 2.

9

went to Trafalgar Square and fed the pigeons
    into the National Gallery to see the pictures
walked to Buckingham Palace and watched the changing of the guard
    across London Bridge and watched the ships and barges
        Blackfriars Bridge and saw the Festival Hall
spent a couple of hours in Battersea Park on the amusements
visited the Houses of Parliament and Westminster Abbey

5	**2**
Regent's Park	visited the Zoo
Earl's Court	saw the Motor Exhibition
the White City	watched the show jumping
	athletics

On the beach

AUNTIE: When the tide comes in, we'll have a bathe.

JACK: How long will it be, Auntie?

AUNTIE: There'll be enough water in about two hours' time. Put your bathing costumes on and collect cockles in the mud.

JILL: Will the water be warm?

AUNTIE: It's often quite warm when there's an afternoon tide on a sunny day. We sometimes stay in for an hour. It won't be cold today.

JACK: Can we go for a sail?

AUNTIE: When you have had your bathe we will eat our lunch and then we can all go for a sail.

JILL: Are we going to have a picnic on the beach? How lovely! We hardly ever have a picnic.

PRACTICE

AUNTIE: If it's fine, we'll stay here all day.

JACK: Can we . . . **1**?

AUNTIE: Yes, after we have had our picnic.

JILL: I love picnics. We never/hardly ever have a picnic in our family.

JACK: . . . **9**, I'm going to . . . **1**.

1

stop in the water long
have another bathe
    a ride on a donkey
go paddling
    fishing on the pier
    to the fun fair
    and see the concert
    in a boat
    out to the wreck
collect shells
play cricket on the beach

9

if it's warm
    sunny
    calm
    not crowded
    wet
when the tide goes out
        comes in

133

At the railway station

PASSENGER: Second class return to Sheffield, please.
TICKET CLERK: That'll be four pounds five.

— . —

PORTER: Where for, sir?
PASSENGER: The ten ten to Sheffield, please.
PORTER: Give me your bags, sir. This way, please. The train is standing at Platform Two. First or second, sir?
PASSENGER: Second class non-smoker, and a corner seat if you can find one.

Brighton.

— . —

PORTER: Here you are, sir. Your bags are on the rack.—Thank you, sir.
PASSENGER: Is it a through train?
PORTER: Yes, sir. Non-stop to Sheffield.

PRACTICE

PORTER: Where for, sir/madam?
PASSENGER: The . . . 5.
PORTER: Give me your suitcase, sir/madam. This way, please. First or second, sir/madam?
PASSENGER: . . . 5a, please.

5		5a	
twelve fifteen to	London	first-class	smoker
two thirty five	Brighton	second-class	non-smoker
	Oxford		sleeper
	Cardiff	pullman	
	Glasgow		
	Birmingham		

In the dress shop

SALESWOMAN: Yes, madam?
MRS SMITH: Evening dresses, please.
SALESWOMAN: This way, please.—We have a good stock of the latest models from Paris.
MRS SMITH: Nothing too expensive, please. That black silk looks attractive. May I try it on?
SALESWOMAN: Certainly, madam. In this cubicle, please.

— . —

SALESWOMAN: It fits madam beautifully.
MRS SMITH: How much is it?
SALESWOMAN: Fifteen pounds, madam.
MRS SMITH: That is rather more than I wanted to pay.

PRACTICE

SALESWOMAN: Yes, madam?
MRS SMITH: . . . 5, please.
SALESWOMAN: This way, please.— We have a good stock of the latest styles.

— . —

MRS SMITH: How much are these?
SALESWOMAN: 5a, madam.

5	5a
gowns	three guineas
hats	four
summer frocks	forty-five shillings
underclothes	five/six/seven pounds
stockings	fifteen and six
dressing gowns	nineteen and eleven
gloves	

In the post office

CUSTOMER: This parcel for Edinburgh, please.

POST OFFICE CLERK: On the scale, please. Ten pence.

CUSTOMER: A twenty five penny book of stamps, please, and a postal order for fifteen pence.

CLERK: That will be fifty one pence altogether, sir.

CUSTOMER: Oh, and can I get a television licence here?

CLERK: Yes, sir. The licence will be four pounds.

CUSTOMER: It's very expensive.

CLERK: It includes the radio licence as well.

This parcel for Edinburgh . . .

CUSTOMER: This parcel for **X**, please.

CLERK: On the scales, please.— That'll be **. . . 5**.

CUSTOMER: And **. . . 5a** and **. . . 5a**, please.

CLERK: That'll be **. . .** altogether. (Do the addition yourself).

5	**5a**

5

twelve pence
two pounds
one pound fifteen
eighteen pence
twenty six pence

5a

a wireless licence (£1)
   dog licence   (37½p)
   gun licence   (50p)

three threepenny stamps (9p)
six   (18p)

a postal order for
   twenty five pence (26p)
   fifty pence   (51p)
   sixty pence   (61p)

On the farm

BILL: What's that big red machine?

FARMER: It's called a combine harvester. It's a machine for cutting corn, the latest model. It cuts the ears of corn and threshes them and feeds the grain to a tender as it goes round the field.

BILL: Can I see it work?

FARMER: If it's fine tomorrow we'll start the harvest. The corn in the big field is ripe. We used to be at the mercy of the weather: sometimes, in very wet weather, a crop was completely lost. Now, in one fine day, a big field of wheat can be harvested and stored away safely.

BILL: Shall I be able to help?

FARMER: Yes, a strong lad like you can be very useful.

PRACTICE

BILL: What's that?

FARMER: That's . . . 5.

BILL: Mother said I was to be useful. Can I help with any of the farm work?

FARMER: Yes, you certainly can. You can . . . 1.

BILL: Good, when shall we start?

FARMER: First thing tomorrow morning.

5

the new milking machine
    trough for dipping sheep
    barn for storing the corn
a machine for baling hay and straw
                grading eggs
    cutter for making cattle food

1

pick peas in the long field
    apples and pears in the orchard
collect eggs for my wife
help move the chicken coops on to the stubble
feed the cattle
work on the straw stack

137

At the police station

MRS BROWN: Oh dear, officer!
I've lost my little dog.
POLICE CONSTABLE: Where
would that be, madam?
MRS BROWN: In the Park. I let
him off the lead while I sat
on a seat to rest. I dozed off
and when I woke up he was
nowhere to be found.
P.C.: What sort of dog is he,
madam?
MRS BROWN: A brown rough-
haired terrier. He answers to
Bingo.
P.C.: Has he got a collar?
MRS BROWN: I'm afraid I took
it off.

I've lost my little dog.

P.C.: It's an offence to let a dog run loose without a collar, madam.
Just give me your name and address and if Bingo turns up we'll let
you know.

PRACTICE

MRS BROWN: Oh dear, officer! I've lost my little dog.
P.C.: What sort of dog is it, madam?
MRS BROWN: A . . . **5**. He/She answers to **X**. I don't know what I
shall do if I can't find him/her.
P.C.: Just give me your name and address, and if it turns up we'll let
you know.

5

peke
small collie
bull terrier
sheepdog puppy
lurcher
corgi bitch
brown rough haired mongrel
dachshund

At the hotel

TRAVELLER: May I have a single room with bath, please?

RECEPTIONIST: We're rather full, sir. Let me see. I can let you have a double room with bath, or a single room without bath.

TRAVELLER: Is the single room a quiet one?

RECEPTIONIST: Yes, sir, very quiet, and there is a bathroom on the corridor nearly opposite.

TRAVELLER: All right, I'll take it, for two nights, please.

RECEPTIONIST: Number 311. Here is your key, sir. The porter will take you and your luggage up in the lift. Would you like to be called?

TRAVELLER: Yes, please, at 8 o'clock, with a cup of tea.

PRACTICE

TRAVELLER: May I have ... **5**, please, with a ... **5a**.

RECEPTIONIST: Certainly, sir/madam. Number ... **4** (and no. ... **4**),

TRAVELLER: Can I/we have ... **5b**?

RECEPTIONIST: Yes, sir/madam // Yes certainly, sir/madam. I'll arrange it.

5		**4**	**5a**
a double room with bath		301	double bed
single-room		411	cot for the baby
a double room and a single next door		219	nice view
two single rooms		126	wireless set
		83	telephone

5b

an early call
    cup of tea
breakfast in my/our room

Note: The usual way of saying numbers over a hundred is, e.g., three owe one (301) four one one (411) one two six (126). Three hundred and one, four hundred and eleven, one hundred and twenty-six are also correct. With numbers under a hundred it is more usual to say, e.g., sixty-five, twenty-nine, eighty-three.

139

In the restaurant

JOHN: Let's sit in the window. Here's an empty table.
JOAN: What a pleasant view! What lovely roses in the garden!
JOHN: Here's the menu. Would you like a drink while we're waiting?
JOAN: Yes, please. Can I have a dry martini?
JOHN: Waiter.—Bring a dry martini and a pint of bitter, please.
WAITER: Very good, sir.

JOAN: I think I'll have tomato juice and the fish.
JOHN: And I shall have tomato soup followed by roast duck.
WAITER: Thank you madam, sir. And what to follow?
JOHN: We'll decide that after the main course.
WAITER: Very good, sir.

PRACTICE

JOAN: I think I'll have . . . 5 followed by . . . 5a.
JOHN: And I'll have . . . 5 and then . . . 5a.
WAITER: Very good, sir. And what to follow?
JOAN: . . . 5b for me, please.
JOHN: And I'll have . . . 5b, please.
WAITER: Thank you, sir, madam.

5	5a	5b
clear soup	roast beef and Yorkshire pudding	meringue
thick soup	roast lamb	rice pudding
smoked salmon	chicken	fruit salad
hors d'oeuvres	turkey	apple tart
pineapple juice	pork	plum tart
orange juice	shepherd's pie	cherry tart
the fish		ice cream
an omelette		a sundae

In the library

MARY: Three books to return.

LIBRARIAN: There's 2½ pence to pay on this one. It's a fort-night overdue.

MARY: Are any of the books on my reserved list in yet, please? My name is Mary Jones.

LIBRARIAN: Yes, Miss Jones, I have kept "Shakespeare's England" for you.

MARY: Oh, thank you. I'll just go and choose two other books.

LIBRARIAN: Good. I'll leave this one by the issue counter.

. . . it met with an accident.

PRACTICE

MARY: Three books to return. May I renew this one, please?

LIBRARIAN: Yes. There's . . . **5** to pay on this one. It's . . . **6** over-due. This one is in rather bad condition.

MARY: I'm afraid it met with an accident.

LIBRARIAN: Then I'm afraid you'll have to pay for the replacement. 25 pence is the set charge. There will be . . . **5** to pay altogether. Now you may choose your new books.

5	**6**
twenty six pence	a week
twenty ninepence	three weeks
thirty pence	a month
thirty four pence	ten days
thirty five pence	
thirty seven and a half pence	

At the door

HOUSEWIFE: Good morning, milkman.

MILKMAN: Morning, mam. Lovely morning, mam.

HOUSEWIFE: Yes, isn't it. I do hope it keeps fine over the weekend. What's the bill this week?

MILKMAN: Sixty pence, mam. Seven pints of grade A, a dozen eggs, and half-a-pint of cream.

HOUSEWIFE: Here you are, one pound. Oh, I forgot. I shall want an extra pint tomorrow.

MILKMAN: Thank you, mam. Forty pence change.

HOUSEWIFE: Thanks. Don't forget to take the empties.

Don't forget to take the empties.

PRACTICE

HOUSEWIFE: What do I owe this week?

MILKMAN: . . . 5, mam, for . . . 5a.

HOUSEWIFE: Here you are. Please bring . . . 5b on Sunday.

MILKMAN: Thank you, mam.

5	5a	5b
forty seven pence	two pints of Grade A milk	two extra pints of milk
thirty nine pence	half a pint of cream	half a pint of cream
sixty four pence	one dozen eggs	one pound butter
seventy seven pence	two pounds of best butter	half a dozen new laid eggs
eighty two pence		

142

At the agricultural show

THOMPSON: I always take a day off for the County Agricultural Show.

JACKSON: So do I, if it is in our part of the County.

THOMPSON: That's a very fine shorthorn bull. Shown by Johnson, I see. I'd like him with my herd.

JACKSON: Yes. It's won first prize. Johnson usually does well with his cattle at the Show.

THOMPSON: Have you seen the sheep? There's a wonderful lot of yearlings on show.

JACKSON: I am more interested in some of the new harvesting machinery. I lost a lot of corn last year in the bad weather.

THOMPSON: My wife is looking at the poultry and rabbits.

PRACTICE

THOMPSON: That's a fine . . . 5 over there.

JACKSON: Yes, I wish mine were as good. Let's go and look at the . . . 5a.

THOMPSON: My wife likes the . . . 5a best.

JACKSON: I like seeing the . . . 5a best of all.

5	5a
cart horse	poultry
pedigree cow	turkeys
heifer	geese
bullock	rabbits
mare and foal	tractors
flock of sheep	ploughs
lambs	cattle
sow	flower-show
boar	farmhouse cooking
litter of piglets	dairy show
	milking machinery

By the river

BILLY: Have you caught anything?
TOMMY: Only a small perch. I haven't been fishing long.
BILLY: Look at that big one, just downstream of that patch of weed.
TOMMY: Yes, I know. Keep still. That's the one I'm after.
BILLY: I'm going to fish a bit further down. What bait are you using?
TOMMY: Worms, but I have some paste as well.
BILLY: Look out! You've got a bite. Your float is bobbing.

PRACTICE

BILLY: Had any luck?
TOMMY: I've got . . . **5** and . . . **5**, and I've only been fishing for an hour.
BILLY: What bait are you using?
TOMMY: . . . **5a**, but I've also brought some . . . **5a**.

5	**5a**
n pike	worms
gudgeon	maggots
chub	gentles
bream	minnows
few minnows	flies
small trout	bits of meat
two dace	paste
roach	bread
three perch	

In the grocer's shop

MRS WHITE: I think that's all for today, thank you. Oh, no! I mustn't forget the butter. Let me have a pound of butter, please.

GROCER: That's on the other counter, mam. Is there anything else you want on this side?

MRS WHITE: Perhaps I'd better take some dried fruit. Let me have a pound of raisins, and half-a-pound of currants. And I'll take a bottle of tomato sauce, and two ounces of white pepper.

— . —

GROCER: Thank you, mam. That will be one pound twenty three all told. Please pay at the desk. If you give me your bag, I'll pack everything in.

PRACTICE

MRS WHITE: I'll have . . . 5 please, and . . . 5, and . . . 5, and . . . 5. That's all, I think.

GROCER: That will be . . . 5a altogether. Please pay at the desk. Goodday, mam.

5

a pound of cheese
                bacon
two pounds of butter
                cooking fat
                sugar
a two pound bag of flour
                self-raising flour
   packet of cake mixture
   packet of salt
                suet
two tins of sausage meat
a tin of pineapple
                peaches
                apricots
                plums
   jar of fish paste

5a

ninety two pence
one pound seventeen
fifty four pence
ninety seven pence
one pound fifteen
one pound forty two
thirty two and a half pence

In the country in spring

MRS BLAKE: Aren't the birds singing beautifully?

MR BLAKE: Yes, they are busy with their nests.

MRS BLAKE: Some of the trees and bushes are already in leaf.

MR BLAKE: The hawthorn and the hazel are usually early, but the oak and the ash are late. Look at this ash—the buds don't seem to have moved at all.

MRS BLAKE: Oh, what a lovely patch of primroses! And here are some violets. Shall we pick a bunch of flowers?

. . . busy with their nests.

MR BLAKE: If you like, but I prefer to leave them growing in the wood.

PRACTICE

MR BLAKE: The . . . 5 is already coming into leaf, but the . . . 5 shows no sign of Spring yet.

MRS BLAKE: Oh! look at those . . . 5a! And here are some lovely . . . 5a. Let's pick a bunch.

MR BLAKE: As you like. I myself prefer to leave them growing in the wood.

5	5a
beech	bluebells
sycamore	harebells
hornbeam	anemones
alder	aconites
willow	celandines
poplar	
birch	
field maple	

146

In the class-room

MASTER: Quiet, now! Get out your Geometry Books. Yes, Peter, what is it?

PETER: Please, sir, may I open the window?

MASTER: Yes, it is a bit stuffy here. Now open your homework on the desk. I am coming round the class to look at it. Meanwhile you can be trying this problem on the blackboard.—Well, Joan, this is not very good. Why haven't you finished your homework?

JOAN: My brother would have the television on last night, sir, and there was nowhere else for me to work.

MASTER: All right. You can stay behind after school and finish it. There's no television here!

PRACTICE

MASTER: Get out your . . . **4** books. Yes, Peter, what is it?

PETER: Please, sir, may I . . . **1**.

MASTER: No, not during my lesson. Now let me look at the homework.—This is not very good, Joan. You had better stay behind after school and do it again.

4	**1**
Latin	sharpen my pencil
Algebra	borrow a pen
Arithmetic	be excused
History	go to see Mr **X**
Geography	close the window
Physics	clean the blackboard
Botany	
English	

In the kitchen

MRS GREEN: It's my turn to wipe up.

MR GREEN: All right, I'll do the washing-up. What a lot of dirty things!

MRS GREEN: Wait a minute. I haven't finished clearing the breakfast things yet.

— . —

MR GREEN: Oh dear! I've broken this cup. It just slipped out of my hand.

MRS GREEN: Do be careful, dear! We shall soon have no cups left.

. . . have no cups left.

MR GREEN: I can't think how we get so many dirty crocks and pans from one meal for two!

MRS GREEN: There are the supper things as well, you know.

PRACTICE

MR GREEN: Oh dear! I've broken it. It just slipped out of my hand.

MRS GREEN: Do be careful, dear! Soon we shall have no . . . **5**s left. Have you done the . . . **5a** yet?

MR GREEN: No. I must have some more water. What a lot of dirty things from one meal!

5	5a
saucer	knives
plate	carving knife
soup plate	forks
small plate	spoons
dessert plate	teaspoons
dish	tablespoons
tea pot	ladle
jug	egg beater
vegetable dish	saucepan
egg cup	

A tea party

MRS FORD: What nice sandwiches! I do so enjoy cucumber sandwiches.

MR WOOD: I am admiring your silver teapot.

HOSTESS: It was my great grandmother's. I keep it for special occasions.—Do you take milk, Mrs Ford?

MRS FORD: Just a little, and no sugar, thank you.

MR WOOD: I would like mine with a little lemon, please.

HOSTESS: You are like me, I see. I prefer lemon with china tea.—Please have a piece of cake.

MRS FORD: Thank you. How nice it looks. Is it home made?

HOSTESS: Yes, I made it yesterday.

PRACTICE

MR WOOD: What nice ... 5. I do so enjoy ... 5.

MRS FORD: I am admiring your ... 5a.

HOSTESS: It belonged to my great grandmother. We only bring it out on special occasions. Do have some more ... 5, Mrs Wood.

MR WOOD: Thank you very much.

5	5a
egg sandwiches	silver tea service
tomato and cheese	china
cake	milk jug
brown bread and butter	silver
currant bread	tea cosy
biscuits	tray
crumpets	lovely table cloth
buttered toast	
pastries	

The picnic

FATHER: This seems a good place, under the tree.

MOTHER: Oh, yes. What a nice view across the valley.

TOMMY: Hurry up with the lunch, mum. I'm terribly hungry.

JILL: So am I. I didn't have much breakfast.

MOTHER: Come on then, all lend a hand. Father, you get the stove going and put the kettle on for the coffee. Jill, spread the cloth and set out the plates. Tommy, open this tin and then pour out the lemonade. I'll cut the sandwiches.

FATHER: We've forgotten the matches.

MOTHER: No, here they are, in the basket.

JILL: Oh dear, there's a wasp!

FATHER: Never mind, it won't hurt you if you don't hurt *it*.

TOMMY: What shall we do if it comes on to rain, Dad?

FATHER: Don't worry about that. The sun will be out again in a moment.

PRACTICE

FATHER: This seems a good place, . . . 7.

MOTHER: Oh, yes. What a . . . 5!—Come on, now; everybody help, Father, you . . . 9; Elsie, . . . 9; John, . . , 9 I'll . . . 9.

7

near the bank of the stream
by the lake
in that field
on the side of the hill
looking south towards the downs
in the wood

5

quiet spot
shady spot
nice bank to sit on
delightful view
good place to fish
               to to play cricket
lot of butterflies

9

get the basket out
collect wood for a fire
spread the rug to sit on
pour out the beer
      soup
      drinks

put the bread   on a plate
     rolls
     sausage rolls
     pasties
fill the kettle
cut the bread and butter

After the pictures

MOTHER: I haven't been to the pictures for months.
JOAN: I haven't been since Easter, until today.
MOTHER: Which cinema did you go to?
JOAN: To the Royal, to see "The Hermit".
MOTHER: What was it like?
JOAN: Not bad. It's about a man who had committed a crime, and thought that nobody knew what he had done, but he didn't know that one person was on his track.
JOHN: I couldn't understand what it was all about. I preferred the Western. The hero, who could ride any horse and was a crack shot, vowed that he would catch the robbers who had stolen his cattle.

PRACTICE

MOTHER: What was the film about?
JOAN: It was about a man/woman who . . . **9**. He/She thought that . . . **9a**.
JOHN: I didn't understand what it was all about. I preferred the first picture. It was about a man who . . . **9**. He vowed that he would . . . **1**.

9

had a strange gift of healing
    great gift of poetry
lived in a dream world
had lost his/her memory

was in love with someone whom
    he/she had only seen once
the owner of a ranch
believed in witchcraft

9a

he/she could work in a hospital
poetry was the greatest of the arts
he/she was really an ancient Egyptian
he/she could remember the past if
    he/she got to a certain place
the loved one was already married

he would steal his neighbours' cattle
he/she could make rain

1

devote his life to helping the sick
get revenge on his brother, who had wronged him
become the chief of a tribe
never marry anyone else
write a great poem
prove the truth of his belief

Index